One room living

Sue Rowlands

a Design Centre book

One room living
First edition published 1977
A Design Centre book published by
Design Council 28 Haymarket
London SW1Y 4SU

Designed by Anne Fisher
Printed and bound by Balding+Mansell Ltd
London and Wisbech

ISBN 0 85072 052 4 (paperback)
ISBN 0 85072 053 2 (hardback)
© Sue Rowlands 1976

Contents

Introduction

The idea of 'living in one room' conjures up either romantic notions of artistic attics and garrets, or just as many un-romantic visions of dingy bed-sits. But for an increasing number of people one room living is no longer a financial or practical necessity. It is a deliberate choice that reflects a new approach to living, and at the same time makes the most of the shrinking space available to us all. Living in a single area is a concept that can be regarded either as a temporary stop-gap en route to more conventional housing, or as a valid philosophy in itself. It is often the first step in self-reliance, and that on its own is an exciting challenge.

Who does it

Although a bed-sit may only be a temporary measure for many students and home leavers, it will be a first place to call their own, a chance to reveal and establish their own style and personality in what may become a warm and happy sanctuary. Newly-marrieds, too, saving for their own bricks and mortar, will often opt for an all-in-one space as their first home – it's a sensible choice as it's cheap to heat, easy to clean and requires the minimum amount of furniture. And no doubt with the first flush of love, any inconveniences will be happily over-looked!

This same warmth and convenience is often sought by an older and more established set of homemakers. Many business people, for instance, live five days a week in one room accommodation and manage easily and conveniently to run a successful business life of enter-

taining, working and sleeping within four apparently restricting walls. Families, too, sometimes find a well designed and separate single room is the answer to the tricky problem of housing aged parents who obviously still value their independence.

The term 'one room living' also encompasses the group of people who choose to live open-plan, either because of increasing building costs or in a fight against the claustrophobia of little boxes. Generally this type of one room living is based on a larger space that has been opened up in an ordinary house, where the increased feeling of light and air make the spaces seem much larger, and where privacy and seclusion are provided only by visual dividers, changes in floor levels and ceiling heights.

Whatever the size and scale of one room living, the pros and cons are roughly the same. The advantages are the versatility, flexibility and freedom of choice that open-plan, all-in-one living space offers; the savings on heat and maintenance; and possible economies in building and land costs. The disadvantages are also clear: one room living can become chaotically out of hand, resulting in a muddle of depressing untidiness, lack of privacy, and total failure to organise space – in fact a complete shambles that doesn't remotely resemble anything like 'home'.

This book is written for people who find themselves making their home within four walls, whatever the shape or size and whatever the circumstances. It's designed to inspire new ideas, but most of all to make you think about sensible solutions to the general problem of living happily in small or open-plan spaces. Some of the suggestions involve major structural improvements and are obviously intended for the committed open-planners. Others are simple, quick and inexpensive tricks that will make life more pleasing and more fun, even for those who see their one room living as a short-term stop-gap.

GEOFFREY FROSH

Opposite: This splendid and unusually designed open-plan home illustrates totally committed one room living. The separate living spaces are created by varying levels, furniture groupings and visual frontiers.
Above: A smaller but equally workable bedsitter is this split-level space where a platform construction provides a capacious sleeping area as well as a working/dining space below.

Planning to make the most of your room

Home, according to the dictionary, means a dwelling place or fixed residence. For most of us, however, 'home' has many more emotional and psychological connotations: it's the warm and welcoming nest; the sturdy, protective 'castle'. Nesting is a natural and instinctive force that affects all of us and makes it easy to understand why so many first-homers rush headlong into heavy mortgages in order to secure for themselves what would appear to be only boxes of bricks and mortar. But homemaking, of course, demands many more home comforts than just this sturdy outer wrapper. The general rule is to begin with the basic necessities for survival and then move cautiously on, developing your taste as finance allows.

Basic essentials
When you're moving into a first home, you'll find that you automatically acquire some ghastly, restricting things called 'priorities'. These priorities will generally incorporate the bare basics of living, sleeping and eating. If you're in a position to buy new furniture, then buy well and selectively, for the rapidly rising costs of home furnishings enforce a long-term policy. A good, well made bed is a sound investment, and investment is the right word, for even the cheapest bed – and that should be one that reaches the minimum requirements of the British Standards Institution – will make a considerable hôle in your budget. Beds are difficult items to buy, for their costly mystique lies deceptively under decorative coverings. It's a fact, however, that if you buy the wrong bed because you've been won over by its good looks, it won't provide you with the ingredients for a good night's sleep. (And you'll know a bad night's sleep, for you'll feel tired, aching and horribly grumpy.) Spend as much as you can on your bed, for although the high price won't necessarily mean that it lasts for ever (expect about twenty to twenty-five years at the most)

it will ensure better support. Try and lie on all the beds in the shop to see how they feel and how you feel. Most reputable stores that sell a wide range will have staff sufficiently experienced to advise you, so tell them at the start what your price range is, and they'll get down to the hard facts rather than wasting time on the sales chat.

An equally demanding priority is a cooker. If your first home is a stop-gap, then the cooker you buy should obviously be a free-standing one rather than a built-in hob and oven arrangement. Although the range of cookers available is enormous, your first limitation will, of course, be the type of power that is on tap to feed it – gas, electricity or solid fuel. The second limitation will be the space available (always measure up accurately before shopping for anything) and also the amount of cash you can spend. Be wary of false economies: my first cooker was a three-burner gas cooker, chosen because it was cheaper than a four-burner one, but I see now that I should have paid the extra because my deprived cooker simply couldn't cope with my inexperienced and disorganised meal preparations. Always try to assess your true needs before shopping so that you have your requirements firmly fixed in your head in case you get side-tracked by good looks and clever salesmen.

Another important need is for a food store of some sort, for even if you shop daily you'll probably need some form of ventilated store. The refrigerator these days has taken over the role of larder and can be seen as an economy measure in that it keeps food fresh for a longer period. If you can afford a fridge, a wise buy is again to choose a happy medium, one that will move on with you and fit any new home with ease. Regardless of the tempting reductions on larger-than-life refrigerators/freezers, give them a miss unless you really need a food store for an entire family. If you choose a moderately sized appliance, one that slips under standard height work surfaces and houses the amount of food you need to store, you will probably find it a much better buy in the long run.

A final basic priority should be your heating. Being warm is essential to comfort; in fact there is nothing worse than feeling miserably cold and not being able to do anything about it. The best heating buys for temporary dwellers are usually the ones that are movable, for any fitted system like central heating or gas fires will become a fixture and consequently the property of the landlord. Storage heaters are pretty heavy to move with you, though it is possible, and most people will prefer the lighter plug-in radiators and various types of spot heaters like electric fires, fan heaters and convectors. Whatever kind of electric heating you decide on, it should be used with a thermostat and time switch for the most economical results. (See pages 26 to 27 for the hard facts on heating and controls.) A number of oil-fired appliances – but only buy ones that comply with the required safety regulations – run efficiently and cheaply, and now look much more attractive. Maintenance of oil stoves is a little extra chore, however.

First principles of planning
Being faced with a single space that has to cope with every aspect of daily life – washing, eating, sleeping, relaxing and working – can be quite terrifying. How, you wonder, is it possible to survive morning moods, daily chores and evening frivolities all within the same four restricting walls? It's not a new problem, though. Anglo-Saxons lived, feasted and slept in their great halls hundreds of years ago, and that one room often housed servants and animals too.

Living in one room can be an enlightening and enjoyable experience, but only if it's well organised, and that means planning and arranging the room to suit your own particular lifestyle. Planning to make the most of a room is not a particu-

larly easy task, however, and it involves careful and comprehensive organisation. To get an overall idea of what you need in the way of furniture, storage and living space, you must first work out precisely all your daily routines, plus any hobbies and interests you may wish to pursue. This may seem rather unnecessary, especially if you think you know what you want already, but it's easy to overlook a daily chore that has become a habit, but with a change of surroundings turns into an obtrusive and problematic bit of drudgery if it hasn't been planned for. So the first planning move, regardless of the size, shape or condition of your room, is to list your every move from morning to night. For instance, do you eat breakfast, come home for lunch, eat out or in at night? Is your room an evening and weekend sanctuary or do you use it throughout the day too? Is your room a work-cum-living area, as a student's might be, or is it a room for the pure pleasure of entertaining, relaxing or just putting your feet up? Do you wash clothes every day or once a week at the launderette? Do you share this single room space, have people to stay, or is it a family room? All these facts, mundane as they may sound, add up to your personal living pattern.

Individual needs
A student, for instance, living in one room, needs to be able to sleep, live, work and entertain in his one space. Ideally, he or she should choose a room that is light and sunny with a pleasant outlook, for some of the day may be spent there with evenings out. The emphasis in this case should therefore be on daytime colour and looks and general convenience for studying.

People who are out at work all day and use their homes mostly at night will need a different emphasis. They will want to have a pleasant place in which to wake up and eat breakfast, an easy place to tidy, and, above all, a cosy place to relax in the evenings, where they can watch television

and maybe entertain a few friends.

Established families and couples who live in large open-plan spaces and follow the usual family pursuits of housework, school homework, children's teas and quiet evening meals, quite obviously need to plan their space more thoroughly. It can be made a bit easier if you take a normal house plan and work out the rationale of its different rooms – why and how it's divided. In this way you can come to some working conclusions about your own requirements in the space available to you.

Here is a checklist of questions to help you assess your own specific needs:
1 Do you live in the room all day, and as an afterthought sleep there too? Or is sleeping the priority with living as the secondary function?
2 Do you cook for yourself, do you entertain or do you normally eat out?
3 Do you need space for working, sewing, painting or any other hobbies?
4 Do you share your one room with other people?
5 Does an entire family live in this single space, with many individual activities?

Allocating space
If you list your requirements honestly, without glamorising or overestimating your needs, you should end up with a fairly clear idea of the way you live and the facilities you'll need for a comfortable existence. It's all too easy at this stage, when you see your life pattern clearly outlined on paper, to want to make idealistic changes. But if you've lived happily in a particular way for some time, it's usually pointless to deceive yourself and waste valuable space on furniture arrangements designed for non-existent future commitments.

The main activities that take place in any home involve the general business of living, eating, sleeping, washing of yourself and clothes, cooking and clearing up after any meals you may prepare. If you're restricted to one room, it's quite

possible to group the first three activities together comfortably, separating the last three from the main living area by means of some kind of room divider (see pages 28–35).

The equipment and furniture you need for these activities will obviously vary according to your budget and personal preferences. For cooking, the basics that most people can get away with in comparative ease and comfort are a run of kitchen units, cooker, sink, refrigerator, and shelves and cupboard storage. For sleeping, a bed with some wardrobe and drawer space. The living area requires a table and chairs, plus maybe an easy chair and a large coffee table, some shelving and cupboards to house china and cutlery, books and treasures. Bathing facilities must include at least a hand-basin and, at best, a bath/shower fitment plus lavatory. If the bathroom is shared, you may have to consider washing in the kitchen area.

Once you've considered this general list of activities and equipment, you'll need to think again about your own preferences when allocating space. People who work all day and use their homes only for relaxing, evening meals and sleeping, plus the odd weekend, will place the emphasis on comfort, so that the bed and a comfy chair will take precedence over a dining table and elaborate cooking area. If, on the other hand, entertaining is your first priority, a well planned kitchen is essential together with a neat dining area if you can afford the space. In a case like this the bed may sometimes double up as soft lounge seating supplemented by lots of large floor cushions – and after a good meal who will criticise? With a family set-up or a shared household there's more than just yourself to consider. A vital factor in a limited and undivided space is privacy, and this is one of the most difficult things to allow for in one room occupied by more than

Opposite and below: These three rooms illustrate quite clearly how, with the minimum of furniture changes and the simplest of constructions, a room can conjure up its own specific style as well as altering the emphasis and priorities of daily living.

one person. Two or more people, though living together, just don't behave as one. It's natural for one person to be tidier or quieter than another – one may like knitting while the other enjoys building canoes. In items of planning, two people sharing are as likely as not to be potentially incompatible, and ideally their home should be larger than a conventional bedsit. However, if you are forced or choose to share, the basic rules still apply and in most cases the living/dining activity will take space precedence over the other necessary functions. Cooking could be compressed into a neat workable run, sleeping quarters either hidden or turned into a lounging area.

Planning your space
If you're really serious about re-jigging the space that you have available you'll need to settle down seriously to some basic planning. As with any space planning, the first step should be to draw out your room to scale, marking in accurately all its irregularities – that is chimney-breasts, fitted cupboards, doors, windows etc. Having done this, you then need to measure accurately the existing pieces of furniture that you either want to keep or are lumbered with, and draw these out to scale on separate pieces of paper. You can then cut out these shapes and juggle around with them on your room plan – it's amazing the workable arrangements you may stumble across. What you must not overlook of course is the flow of daily movement and activity. You may imagine you've worked out the most incredible space-saving solution only to find that you can't actually open doors or that you end up sitting comfortably staring at the washing up. Once you feel you've cracked the problem, try it out in practice – generally a small amendment will be necessary but a better workable arrangement may result.

In small do-it-all spaces compromises must be made and these are covered in detail in the chapter on Spacemakers. It's not unusual for beds, because of their overpowering size, to have to double up as seating. If they are to do this regularly, however, the mattress will need to be turned and changed around to keep the support even, and a cushion backrest will make sitting more comfortable. Tables, too, should be bought as multi-purpose items – they need to be versatile enough to be dined at in style, to be cooked on and worked at. Chairs should be selected for use at the table as well as providing comfortable relaxers. Multi-purpose storage systems that house just about everything you use and wear are good one-room remedies – it's much more sensible to have an all-in-one unit rather than a separate wardrobe, the odd wall shelf and a separate chest of drawers. Even if you are lumbered with separate items, it would still be better to group them together – for convenience as well as for a neat streamlined look.

Lighting is discussed in detail on page 27 but a couple of points are worth remembering at the initial planning stage. Spotlights are always a good investment, whether wall fixed or in a standard lamp version, for they can be swivelled around to direct light on any chosen area for different activities. And pendant fittings that rise and fall are useful mood changers – high up they give good all-over lighting, lowered they accentuate and strengthen the light to focus attention on one specific area.

As you start living in and getting to know your one room, you'll no doubt discover extra improvisations that are peculiar to you and your way of living. As long as they make living easier, that's fine, but just make sure that the final arrangement serves you and that you don't have to fit your life around it.

Cans and cannots

Making a home for oneself quite obviously involves much more than just the tedium of finding a flat and moving in. Homes are created by individual people who introduce their own specific requirements, priorities and idiosyncracies. More often than not, people making their home in one room will be attempting to create their own very personal and intimate nest within the confines of rented and often furnished property – a hard task when you consider how difficult it is to make up your own mind about furnishings and decoration, let alone having to work within the framework of someone else's ideas! Nevertheless, the situation exists and, strangely enough, it really can take only the smallest arrangement of personal treasures or the addition of one extra fixture to make life much more pleasant and your 'home' a very special place.

So, if you want to personalise your one room, just what are you allowed to do? You may have unlimited ideas but your landlord could have a very restricting view on the subject. Even if you own your room or open-plan space the freedom to change things, although obviously greater, is nevertheless limited by safeguarding laws and local authority regulations. So here to start with are some broad guidelines on what you can and cannot do.

Rented accommodation
Since 1968, tenants of unfurnished property have been protected by the Rent Act and since 1974 this same Act has been extended to protect tenants of furnished properties too, where the landlord is resident. Quite reasonably this protection is a two-sided affair, for the landlord also must have some freedom within his property. For a tenant, however, the Act's protection means that the landlord can only evict you if he can satisfy a court of law that he has very good and acceptable reasons as laid down by the Act. One of the most common reasons for eviction is failure to pay rent, but a reasonable court may allow you to correct the situation – in effect by paying up and continuing to do so. Other causes for eviction are creating a nuisance or annoying other people within the property, and damaging the premises, which includes the furniture in the case of furnished accommodation. You can also be asked to leave if you are housing too many people in your room, or if the landlord wants the space to house himself or a relative of his. However, as a protected tenant you don't have to leave if you simply have notice to quit. The only way a landlord can remove you is by obtaining a County Court possession order and if you receive one of these or a notice to leave you should seek advice, possibly from your neighbourhood law centre, housing aid centre or your local Council's legal division.

If you do receive notice to quit, you may be able to get this deferred by making an application to the Rent Tribunal, which can give you up to six months' security of tenure at any one time. The Rent Tribunal's address can be obtained from the Citizens Advice Bureau, your local Council, or the telephone directory.

If your landlord lives on the premises or you are provided with some sort of board – such as breakfast or an evening meal – you are most probably not a protected tenant under the Act. This means, basically, that you have to live according to the landlord's own 'rules' and you should therefore regard the accommodation as a short-term stay – unless, of course, it's superbly comfortable and the food's better than mother could provide, in which case you should count your blessings! Tenants of rented accommodation should always be aware of their legal position. Tussles with landlords may never occur, but it's well worth knowing what your rights are, especially since you may be so keen to make a home of your one room that you won't want to part with it or be forced in any way to leave.

What can be done

Most structural alterations, but possibly not decoration, will need the permission of your landlord. Even putting up the simplest shelf, for example, could technically put your home in jeopardy because it could be interpreted as damaging the property and, consequently, a reason for eviction – although a court might just ask you to take it down and make good the wall. The term 'structural' is not as major as it sounds because it is often used to define less drastic alterations to a house, like removing a flimsy partition wall, fitting extra wiring points, plumbing-in washing machines and so on, as well as the more expensive and complex jobs like installing central heating, adding an extra bathroom or knocking two rooms into one.

The best thing is always to discuss your plans with your landlord. Most sensible landlords, and certainly the shrewd ones, will be only too happy for you to improve their property at your own expense. To safeguard yourself legally, however, you must get permission in writing and at the same time submit any relevant drawings and plans for the project. If the alterations are extensive you may, of course, need additional permission from the local authority. In most leases there is a clause that states that, while the landlord must give his permission for any alterations, he is at the same time not entitled to withold his consent unreasonably. If a landlord's refusal appears to be unreasonable it would be as well to take legal advice before challenging his decision. It would be foolish to carry out the work secretly in the hope of never being discovered, because landlords, inquisitive or otherwise, are allowed to enter your room to inspect it or carry out repairs providing that they give at least one day's notice. You can imagine that any case of deliberate defiance leaves a court with no way of saving you from losing your home.

Council tenants, similarly, should ask the Council's permission to install even a bookshelf, let alone a fitted wardrobe or storage system, and more often than not this permission will be granted as a matter of course. The need for permission is not simply a question of irritating red tape for its own sake – it provides a safeguard for the property, especially where newly-built homes are concerned. Many new council houses and flats, for instance, are built with modern materials like fair-faced concrete that just won't bear the weight of heavy units fixed to the wall with screws. The Council must also safeguard the services that supply power and water to flats and which would cause chaos if accidentally severed. A number of clued-up councils now provide their tenants with general instruction manuals that give details of what can be put up where and how.

Once you have got permission and built your fitments you've provided your landlord with extra 'fixtures and fittings'. Basically, everything that is attached to a wall is technically known as a fixture or fitting and consequently becomes the landlord's property. Strictly speaking, these fixtures and fittings should be left behind when you move on. Lenient landlords and some councils will, in fact, allow you to take some fixtures with you on condition that you make good any holes in walls and leave everything looking presentable. Fireplaces are also regarded as fixtures, so if you replace an old inefficient gas fire with a spanking new one you'll have to leave that behind – unless you keep the old fire and have it swopped back – and the same applies to a stone or metal fire surround. So unless you intend to live in the same place for a considerable length of time it's an extravagance to replace a monstrosity of this sort when a bit of thoughtful camouflage could well do the trick instead. Fixtures and fittings can, of course, be sold by the out-going tenant or the landlord. If you are in a position to buy them you should insist on a complete, priced inventory and, assuming the prices are not excessive, the deal should go through smoothly with fair returns for both parties and no come-backs later on. If you think the prices are extortionate, however, you can call on the help of the local Council, who have the power to inspect the items in question and will presumably judge fairly.

Overall, the basic codes are the normal social ones of consideration and courtesy. If you consider the feelings of your neighbours then you can and should expect equal consideration in return if you're troubled or annoyed in some way, and you can ask for their co-operation with a clear conscience. And, when looking after and making changes to your rented home, always bear in mind that it's someone else's bricks and mortar and remember how you'd feel if it were your own. The law falls fairly on both sides and if you have a gripe or feel you're not getting a fair deal, a trip to the Citizens Advice Bureau could help you sort things out.

Owning your own home

Actually owning the shell of your home does have a number of advantages in terms of the freedom it gives you to decorate, replace and alter things in the comforting knowledge that you're improving your lot and, hopefully, increasing the value of your property. This freedom isn't total, however, in so far as improvements of any major kind must be approved by different local authorities, not with the intention of restricting you to mundane schemes, but to ensure that overall good looks are maintained and that your home and those of your neighbours are safe, with sufficient light, air and correct sanitation.

If you want to make major changes – and if you want to make a conventionally segmented property into an open-plan one this will certainly be the case – you may need to employ the services of an architect. A good architect should be able to translate your requirements into a well designed, practical and safe environment.

He will design the complete project, oversee building work and cope with the sporadic visits of the building inspector. If you're attempting to do it yourself you may still find it useful to make use of an architect's services at the planning stage, in which case you'll be paying for his advice on whether the project is a feasible one and also which authorities you need to contact. In fact, you can buy as much or as little of an architect's time as you need and, on more adventurous improvements, you may find it more economical in terms of time and money to employ one to draw up plans and guide you through the maze of necessary permissions. Remember though that advice isn't free, so always agree fees at the outset – they are often calculated on an hourly rate – before enthusiastically involving a specialist.

Before embarking on any major alteration or construction you must consult your local council. It's best to begin with the borough surveyor's department, for here they will be able to tell you just what you can and cannot do, what permissions you will need and – if you're lucky enough to get a nice, helpful soul – you may be guided through the complexities of planning permissions and building regulations. These two controls, however frustrating you may find them, are designed to protect you and your neighbours as well as maintaining a well-balanced overall environment. Planning permission is concerned with the way in which land is developed and the department involved will be interested in things that affect the appearance of the exterior of your house and whether they affect or devalue your neighbours' property in any way. Large extensions over 115 cubic metres, and loft conversions that project or alter the original roof line will need planning permission, so will front porches, as they affect the appearance of the house, and even some walls and fences come into this category. It's as well to get the go-ahead before you start building, even if you think it's not really necessary or rather too much of a performance, because it's quite within the authorities' power to ask you to remove the new structure. Building regulations deal with safety and act as a safety check on the design and construction of new buildings and alterations. Irritating as they may seem, they are designed to protect you and your neighbours' property and sanitation. Plans and specifications of your project will have to be submitted to this department and they will check that the scheme is sound and won't affect the main services, that it won't fall down around you or, even more important, cause a whole row of houses to collapse. Once your plans have been passed and building begins, you must still have the work overseen by a building inspector whose job it is to see that each stage of the work is carried out correctly and well. It's up to you, the householder, to make appointments for his visits – the system will be explained to you – and if you progress beyond a certain stage without his approval he can require you to take the further stage of building down.

Many of the classic open-plan conversions and alterations will need building regulation approval even if they don't need planning permission, and many will need both. Knocking two rooms into one, for instance, usually involves the demolition of walls that are load-bearing – meaning that they are essential to the strength of the structure of the house – and in this case you will be required to reinforce the structure by inserting a steel joist across the gap. A bed shelf structure or a mini minstrel gallery built on stilts, however, may just need some expert advice on strength, materials and construction from an architect or a professional builder, and the same goes for raising a floor level. The only restriction on projects of this type is that the ceiling height in living spaces must be 2285mm or more. Another important regulation, which affects all householders but especially open-planners, is that a lavatory must have a 'lobby', or at least two doors, between it and any area used for cooking or storing food. This is a perfectly reasonable rule for health reasons and is not too much of a problem to plan around.

Doing it yourself is increasingly becoming a financial necessity for most of us and it is well worth while if more space or an individual style is the aim. Happily the interest in do-it-yourself has given rise to a rash of very informative, sensibly illustrated manuals that take one through quite major projects as well as more mundane maintenance, and reading any of these books would be a good way to start. It's quite feasible to attack a great many home alterations yourself, but it's always advisable to get advice and, of course, permission before you start – it's a total waste of time, effort and money if your construction falls down or, even worse, has to be demolished because you didn't stick to the rules and regulations.

Basic essentials

If you ever have cause to ponder on just what constitutes a desirable feeling of well-being, you'll probably end up with a list of basic, day-to-day things that we generally take for granted – a place to cook and to feed oneself and friends, somewhere to bath and wash clothes, and, of course, the luxury of being comfortably warm and dry.

The majority of us have most, if not all, of these basics in some form or other. Yet many of us, especially if we live in one room among inherited chaos or are only able to afford the minimum in the way of necessities, would question whether our own arrangements could even remotely measure up to any standards of efficiency – never mind luxury. This chapter is specifically about these basic essentials. Style and decoration are important, but here I want to show how a bit of planning and modification can help to make your everyday chores more pleasant and smooth running.

Cooking in one room

Cooking food and eating it are, of course, among the most basic human activities – and for many people they make up one of the most pleasurable pastimes as well. Cooking can be seen as a creative and fulfilling means of self-expression, or it may be thought of as a tedious and messy bore, but either way, some sort of kitchen is a necessity in any home. Kitchens are often the despair of many an interested cook – some find their size and shape frustrating, others can't cope with their jumble of equipment, and of course in some rented accommodation the collection of cast-offs can be very off-putting. But there are, in fact, very few problem kitchens that can't be radically improved – their salvation usually depends almost entirely on sensible and logical planning and maybe a little inspiration.

Kitchen planning

Whether you live and cook in one room, own a vast country-style kitchen, or feel you cook in a cupboard, the basics of planning a convenient and well organised work-space are just the same. If you know and understand the logic of kitchen planning there's no reason why you shouldn't be able to apply it to any kitchen you own.

Basically, kitchen planning depends on plotting out a logical working sequence to save the time, energy and mileage that the cook must expend when making a meal. The classic arrangement is a triangular one that encompasses all the preparation, cooking and serving involved. The sequence is : store/wash and prepare/cook and serve, with all these three areas linked by runs of worktops. Of course there are some kitchens that can't be neatly adapted to this sequence, but you can still arrive at something adequate using the rule as a guide. It makes sense, for instance, to store foodstuffs close to preparation areas and to have the sink next in line to provide an area for wet preparation jobs and for washing up. The next stage is cooking and, ideally, the sink and the cooker should be linked by a worktop. This can have a built-in chopping board or a slab for pastry making, which can also be used to rest hot pans on, or it can be a straightforward stretch of plastics laminate. There should also be a final run of worktop on the other side of the cooker to form a serving area and this should logically be as close as possible to the dining area, or at least near the door to the dining room. Above, under and around this central production line there must be adequate space to store everything you need for preparing meals – dry and perishable foodstuffs, pots and pans, washing-up equipment, possibly the china and glassware, cutlery and so forth – and of course each of these should be kept as near to where they're needed as possible.

In many rented rooms, as well as some newly-built homes, you will be stuck with fixtures like sinks, cooker sockets and gas taps that can't or shouldn't be moved, so

these will just have to form the basis for your design. Even a landlady's conglomeration of cooking equipment can be reshuffled into some more efficient order. It's easiest to plan or replan your kitchen area by mapping the kitchen accurately on squared paper, marking in all fixtures and irregularities in the room. You can then draw out all the equipment you own, again to scale, cut out the shapes and place them on the plan. You can then see quite easily what will fit where – and it's much easier than pushing real pieces of furniture around!

As with any planning situation, if you can spot the problem you're half way to tackling it, or at least improving it. If your one room kitchen space is impossible, start by reshuffling it if you can, then cheer it up with some colourful fittings

A one-wall kitchen that contains all the basic necessities for an efficient cooking space. The appliances and fitments run in a logical and workable sequence of washing, preparation and cooking of the food.

and new pots and pans. Old, worn work surfaces can be improved out of all recognition with self-adhesive PVC or, as a more long-term measure, vinyl sheet flooring or a patchwork of vinyl tile oddments. Gaps between units can be bridged with chipboard or chopping surfaces. Ugly walls can be disguised with trellis (good for hanging gadgets on), sheets of foil or even lengths of waxed shelf paper. Just add your own personal touches with conviction and the space will be much more inviting.

A tiny kitchen that works efficiently simply because of initial sensible planning. The walls are used for storage of equipment and food, the L-shaped worktop for the basic sequence of washing, preparing and cooking.

Space making

The most common problem that faces many of us, especially people who live and cook in a single room or maybe within a sort of alcove, is shortage of space. Small kitchens can, in fact, be supremely convenient with everything more or less at hand and because their small size demands a lot of discipline they can present a good, neat appearance as well. But, as with any limited area, you will have to look for as much usable space as possible, and that means making imaginative use of walls and ceilings. These days most fitted kitchens make use of wall space as a matter of course, either with wall-hung cupboards or a total storage wall into which all the appliances – refrigerator, dishwasher, oven, washing machine and so on – can slot. Needless to say, this sort of plan is quite expensive. Plain shelves, however, can look pretty as well as being practical if carefully arranged, and you can also fit brackets and bars to hold kitchen utensils, knives, bunches of herbs and so on. Ceilings are useful for hanging high-level storage shelves or sturdy bars with butchers' hooks to hold all those cumbersome large items like big pans, colanders, sieves etc – they obviously need to be positioned carefully to prevent constant head-banging.

The undersides of shelves can also be fitted with wire drawers or hanging bars and the insides of cupboard doors can carry small, narrow things like spice jars, cleaning cloths and, of course, purpose-built rubbish containers.

Below and opposite: This small kitchen alcove adjoining a dining room space uses its capacious and very necessary storage shelving as a decorative viewpoint for the diners, and at the same time leaving the worktop free for easy and efficient food preparation.

Small space equipment

If you're stuck with a small working area you can either fit it out more or less conventionally with standard-sized fittings, in which case it's likely to feel cramped and possibly rather disorganised, or you can plan in miniature, selecting scaled-down appliances and equipment that will give maximum service for their minimum size. Planning a scaled-down kitchen takes a great deal of research, scrupulous measurement and detailed planning. The result, however, can be an enjoyable place in which to work with everything just where you want it.

Small-scale equipment is manufactured and it can be found, but you probably won't stumble across it in your local electricity or gas showrooms. However, you may be able to get hold of some detailed catalogues and from these you can make a selection and plan your workable kitchen. As with any design project, but particularly when space is short, you must assess your priorities. For people who cook in a cupboard the bare necessities for washing up and cooking may be sufficient, while for others a cold food store will be an essential. List what you need, list what you can buy, and then scale it down to fit the space available – it can be quite an absorbing pastime!

Several kitchen appliance manufacturers make smallish products that are specifically designed for the small-scale kitchen. In addition, many manufacturers for specialist markets, like caravans and boats where space is even tighter than a bed-sit, make useful products, and some others provide small stuff simply to fill a gap in the market of 'bigger and better' appliances that only fit into luxurious spaces.

Cookers are perhaps the most versatile area, for you can buy cooker hobs separately and, if you want, site the oven elsewhere. Or you can buy a free-standing small oven and grill with radiant top rings – these can be bought in combination or as separate items and one small

Left: If space in the kitchen is really tight, a table-top cooker may be the only model which will fit in. The Electra Minorcook is 420mm high, 457mm wide and 355mm deep, and works off a 13 or 15 amp power point. The radiant rings serve for both boiling and grilling, and there is a thermostatically controlled oven.

Floor-standing cookers, both gas and electric, are available in narrow models.

Below left: The Jackson Trimline, 457mm wide, by Creda Electric Ltd.

Below: The Main Malvern gas cooker, 508mm wide, one of the British Gas Superflame range of appliances.

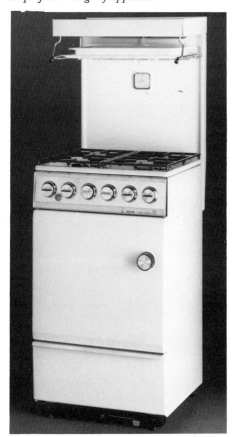

oven can either stand on a worktop or be wall mounted. If there's room for the normal type of floor-standing cooker you should search out the narrowest model – the smallest I know of is only about 45cm wide but it's big enough to cope with family meals. If you eat at home only occasionally you can probably get away with a small grill and hob unit.

Refrigerators too, now they have become necessities, can be found in varying shapes and sizes. Again, you can find standard models that fit under a worktop but are narrower than usual – but do check before buying that the dimensions allow you to open that very fat door! One of the narrowest in the medium-sized category is only about 47cm wide. Others sit neatly on a work-top or fit onto a wall and if they have two star frozen food compartments they can keep quick meals on tap for several days. If there's insufficient space for even a small domestic fridge, look at the ones in caravan supply shops and other specialist space-savers. There are top-opening models that run off either battery or mains and will slip neatly into a space about 43cm square. Freezers come in small sizes too – initially designed to fit on top of an existing refrigerator, but they can just as well be used on their own.

Dishwashers are mostly rather conventional designs in that they are still, comparatively speaking, luxury items – consequently they're produced to the scale of a luxury-sized kitchen. However, some models can stand on a worktop and are relatively small – though even these are rather cumbersome and take up a lot of space in a small kitchen.
A space-saving appliance that saves energy as well is the pressure cooker. This isn't a new cooking idea but a truly tried and tested one – many cooks swear by them. Pressure cookers cook food fast and, as it's cooked under pressure in a closed space, it retains all the flavour and juices too. For anyone with only a small cooker or perhaps a single ring, a pressure

A selection of other space-saving appliances ideal for a small kitchen.
Top: The Electrolux 210 refrigerator is 575mm high, 486mm wide and 457mm deep, and has a net capacity of 48·11 litres. It can be wall hung or sit on a worktop or floor stand. The door can be hung from the left- or right-hand side.
Above left: The Hotpoint Iced Diamond 27020 is a compact four-star freezer which will sit on a worktop or refrigerator. It is 490mm high, 545mm wide and 590mm deep, and has a net capacity of 51 litres. It has a two-speed thermostat control and can take up to 16·3kg of frozen food.
Below left: Pressure cookers cook an entire meal in one pot on a hob. As they cook quickly, they use less fuel. The Prestige Hi-dome has a capacity of 7 litres. (28·3 litres = 1 cubic foot.)

cooker could be a boon as an entire meal can be prepared in just one pot.

Cooking without a cooker

The rising cost of energy has had more effect on the design of small kitchen appliances than all the pleas of the space-starved. The result is a rash of neat little appliances that are called table-top cookers – which is exactly what they are – and you can understand what a boon they are for bed-sits with minimal facilities.

Not a new idea but nevertheless still a very practical and versatile one is the skillet – generally an electrically heated deep pan that is capable of steaming, stewing. frying and even baking (though not all at once, of course) – with which a well organised cook could produce a complete meal. Rather similar is the electric casserole which will cook soups and stews very slowly – all day even – and which is particularly good at making the most of cheap cuts of meat without using a lot of electricity.

There are also a number of neat one-ring grillers that can cope with quite adventurous cooking as both grill and hot-plate can be used simultaneously – all you have to do is organise the timing. One of the trimmest models is a lidded one that's

only about 15cm high, and 38cm in width and depth, so it can be snugly stored away when mealtimes are over. There are also several 'snack' gadgets that will cater quite adequately for the occasional meal at home. Their use is sufficiently limited to make daily meals a bit boring, though, for most of them are intended only to grill meat or toast sandwiches quickly. Along the same lines, but possibly more versatile, is the oven/grill/rotisserie which, as its name suggests, will spit-roast, roast or grill. Again, it's a bit limited and anyone who has to rely entirely on a table-top cooker needs imagination and energy to make meals and cooking interesting.

1

2

3

4

5

1 The Sunbeam Electric 280mm Deluxe Coloured Multi-Cooker will fry, braise, stew, roast, bake, boil and steam. The pan has a non-stick finish and the lid is on a ratchet.
2 The Tower Slow Cooker is an electric casserole which cooks slowly and gently.

Ideal for soups, stews and puddings, it can be left to cook unattended for up to 10 hours using no more power than a light bulb.
3 Moulinex oven/grill/rotisserie will spit-roast, roast or grill. It is a compact table-top cooker, but calls for imaginative cooking as shown here.
4 The Haddock Horstman Speedgrill is portable and works off a 13 or 15 amp power point. It has a high-speed, self-cleaning element, and a five-speed thermostat control for accurate even heat. It acts as a grill or a hotplate.
5 The thermostatically controlled Tefal Grill Barbecue is handy for cooking steaks and chops. It has a large non-stick-coated plate which removes for easy cleaning.

Washing in one room

Washing both yourself and your clothes may have to be catered for when planning your one room. Generally, bathing is kept to a separate bathroom whereas clothes washing can be slotted in to either the kitchen or bathroom or utility room area – wherever it happens to fit in best. The totally committed open-planner who owns his or her own space will most probably want to design all these areas to meet specific needs. Even so, however, an entirely separate area may be considered to be more desirable. By law, you must separate the lavatory from the cooking area by a lobby or at least two doors and, as a bathroom often incorporates a lavatory, this is the function that's most likely to be treated separately. Bed-sitter and flat dwellers often don't have much control over the planning and arrangement of this area, of course, and again they will have to compromise and be inventive. A great many people who live this way will, for instance, have to share a bathroom with other tenants – which can work if everyone pulls their weight, but not if one or two are inconsiderate enough to leave their tide-marks for the next in line. If the bathroom is really unpleasant you may have to consider washing both yourself and your clothes within your own room – perhaps in the kitchen area – and visiting friends when you want the luxury of a hot bath!

Planning a bathroom

Bathrooms are often the most ill-considered and overlooked spaces for they're still frequently thought of as clinical, purely functional spaces. All too often they are cold and wet – places to be suffered rather than enjoyed – and this is particularly true in many rented flats. Part of the reason why bathrooms are put up with and not replanned is the difficulty of moving the big, weighty fittings – plus the vital factor of the expense of re-plumbing. If you own your own home you may consider it's worthwhile, but most one-room dwellers will have to accept the situation, work around it and add bits where they can be fitted in and afforded.

As with any planning, you must start off by considering what you want from the room, bearing in mind its size, shape and potential. For instance, you may want the washing area to house the laundry and clothes-washing equipment too, or you may decide to discard the bath and replace it with a space-saving shower. Even if space is very tight you may still want to have a place for medicines and toiletries. To help you to see things more clearly it's again a good idea to draw a plan of the room to scale, together with the fittings, and then juggle them about objectively. If you're planning from scratch you will have to start off by listing your requirements and priorities – bath size and shape, shower, bidet, basin, lavatory and, possibly clothes-washing facilities. If you're just rearranging you should list the changes you can afford to make plus any extra items you would like to fit in. In each case, you can finish by working on the little personal touches you would like to introduce.

A new idea that one imaginative manufacturer has come up with is the fitted bathroom. It's designed on the same principle as fitted kitchen and bedroom furniture – many items in the range have lids so that they can be used for seating and most match up in height to give a neat appearance, with the square modules forming a complete bank along a wall. This sort of idea can be developed in your own arrangement – fittings can be linked by slatted or plain seating which

The smart lidded units in this fitted bathroom camouflage the fittings and give a streamlined look. The idea can be adapted to provide seating and worktops in a small area. Magnum by Metlex Industries Ltd.

can hide the linen basket, cleaning materials, spare towels and so on. Ordinary shelves, too, can provide a lot of extra space – over windows, at the end of the bath or along its length. Vanitory type handbasins can be fitted into plastics laminate worktops and give added storage space that is ideal for hiding unsightly necessities.

Visually at any rate, bathrooms no longer need to be the cold and clinical rooms they once were. Today they're regarded much more as pleasant, relaxing places and to create this sort of atmosphere you need to develop a warm and personal style. This can be done, not just in the choice of colour scheme, but much more in the selection of accessories – towel rails or rings, towels themselves, taps, shower fittings, even the bathroom scales (there used to be lovely ones that looked like a lawn strewn with daisies, which were really fun). So the formula is to plan the basics, look out for spare spaces, choose your style and then make the most of it.

Space-making fittings

Whether you live in one room or a 'conventional' house, space is always at a premium and, for some obscure reason, the bathroom often gets the meanest share of what's going. If you're short of space but still want a 'proper' bathroom with all the trimmings there are several space-making solutions. Baths, for example, come in many different shapes and sizes. Apart from the standard type you can get ones that fit into a corner, look enormous and do, in fact, probably take up as much useful room as the normal kind. You can also get shorter than standard models that are quite big enough to lounge in, if not at full length; and a more space-saving design is the tub type – virtually a deep, square bath that you sit in and can use as a shower tray too. Showers are particularly economical so far as space and hot water are concerned and many people prefer them. They are

available as complete cabinet units ready for plumbing in or as separate wall-mounted units that can be combined with a shower tray and a curtain. Splashes aren't always contained completely so it's best to surround the shower with washable or wipeable wall and floor coverings. A traditional compromise is the shower unit within a bath – either as a permanent, wall-mounted fixture or a hand-held attachment that can be slotted into a wall bracket. Glass or acrylic shower doors are an alternative to the shower curtain. An absolute boon for a bath area within a multi-purpose space are the box-like structures that are made to enclose showers. They are a bit claustrophobic, but they are private and certainly waterproof. The current emphasis on saving energy has resulted in a number of shower units that contain their own water heaters – they're efficient and can, in fact, save on fuel bills as well as being relatively cheap to install. Finally, the standard pedestal washbasin takes up a lot of space and can often be replaced by a vanitory basin in a worktop. Alternatively, handbasins can be obtained that fit into corners or are recessed into the wall, solving a problem if space is really short.

Clean camouflage

If your bathroom is shared, inherited or just horrible, a good scrub is often the best first shot at a remedy – both baths and basins take on a new look if water stains can be removed or minimised. Stubborn stains get better if rubbed with vinegar or lemon juice and then rinsed, or alternatively treated with proprietary bath cleaners. If the bath's finish is irretrievable, a new coat of paint can improve things – ordinary polyurethane gloss will work on a well cleaned, non-greasy surface and you can also buy special bath enamels. Horrendous lavatories can look positively sparkling after treatment with bleach, and if stains are very stubborn spirits of salt can work

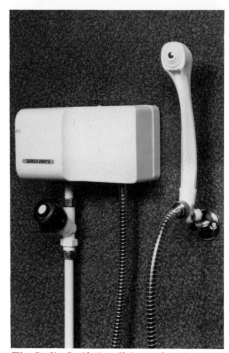

The Sadia Swift 6 wall-hung electric shower fitting gives instantaneous hot water.

wonders, but take care and read the instructions. If after all this the bathroom still looks characterless then fill it with colour with bright towels and toiletries. Plants do well in a steamy atmosphere and will happily decorate a sparse room, and a collection of junk shop mirrors will add a sparkle.

Water heating

If you're lucky, lovely hot water will be provided constantly from a central heating system. More often than not, however, tenants of single rooms will find that landlords have fitted pay-as-you-use gas or electric water heaters. The most common of these are the multi-point gas heaters that will heat water instantaneously for baths and kitchen use. These days, balanced flue heaters of this type can be neatly hidden away in a cupboard. Immersion heaters use electricity to heat and store water, with a thermostat to keep the temperature constant. They can be expensive to run but a thick insulating jacket helps to keep the heat in. Instantaneous electric water heaters just heat the water as you need it – most only produce sufficient water for basins and sinks rather than baths, but special shower models are available. In a large open-plan home hot water is likely to be provided from a central heating system of some sort, but an immersion heater should still be installed for use in the summer.

Clothes washing

Somewhere in your one-room space you may have to wash clothes and dry them. The launderette round the corner has solved many a soggy and dripping problem, but there will still be some items that need to be hand washed and carefully handled. For the homemaker whose one room is permanent, a plumbed-in washing machine and clothes drier could be worthwhile investments in terms of both time and money. Even for the temporary one-room dweller the equipment might be useful as a long-term buy if it can be plumbed in easily. If you have been able to plan your space from scratch you will, no doubt, have designed it to accept the appliances you want, which means you can choose from whatever machines fit your space and your pocket. Fully automatic machines are expensive but can cope with the whole wash from start to finish – some will even dry the clothes as well and, though these are rather less efficient than two separate washing and drying machines, they do take up less space. Semi-automatics need a certain amount of overseeing and manual control, but they are cheaper. All front-loading machines can be permanently plumbed in under a worktop and therefore don't need to be moved out at all. Twin tub machines are generally more cumbersome – they wash, rinse and spin

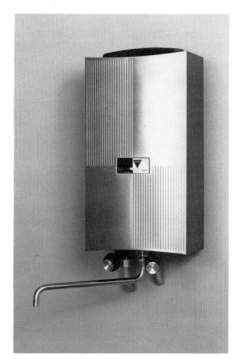

dry, but clothes have to be transferred by hand from tub to tub.

There are also mini, scaled-down washing machines designed to cater for the single person with little washing or for homes that are short of space. A typical model will wash about 1 kg of clothes at a time (a big machine will manage about 4kg) and measures only about 380 × 500 × 500mm. It fits a conventional twin tub system into a small space by enabling each tub to be separated and stored singly.

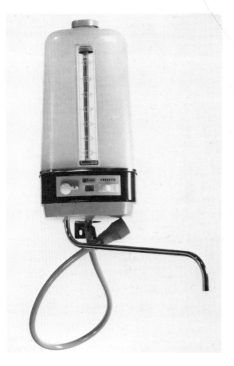

Left: The Ascot 527 instantaneous gas water heater can provide hot water either through the spout only, or supply a shower or wash basin as well.
Right: The Creda Corvette is a handy wall-hung water heater which will boil enough water for a pot of tea in only two minutes. It needs no plumbing in, just a cold tap, and works off a 13 or 15 amp power point.

Clothes drying

If you can't afford the space or the cash for a washing machine, you might still find a spin drier useful. Dripping clothes are a bore, especially in winter, and they're always inconvenient. Neat, tuck-away models can be kept under a work top or in a cupboard and all will get washing to a damp or iron-dry state. Tumbler driers, which use warm air to dry clothes completely or partially, take the process a stage further. There are also a number of quite efficient clothes driers that fold up when not in use. In their simplest form these are plastics-covered wire clothes-horses that straddle a bath. Just as simple, but rather more permanent, are the pull-out clothes-lines that can be fixed above a bath, and the flap-down racks that fold against the wall when not in use.

Heat-assisted clothes driers come in different forms, shapes and sizes. The established method is to have a cabinet which is basically an electrically heated box fitted with a rack to support the clothes. These look neat and can be fitted under work surfaces. Some are claimed to be manoeuvrable enough to take to holiday homes. Other driers use a fan heater to help blow the washing dry. One of the neatest of these fits on a wall, so it doesn't take up any floor space when in use, and folds away when it's not needed. The clothes are hung on rails in a large, zip-up polythene sack and drying times can be pre-set.

Ventilation

Good ventilation helps to keep a home smelling sweet and comparatively condensation and fug-free. Kitchens and bathrooms are often the main trouble spots and in a one-room or open-plan space efficient ventilation is vital.

Efficient ventilation should remove steam and smells fast and create sufficient air movement to prevent stuffiness – in office buildings and some of the better-considered domestic schemes it's bracketed under the heading of air

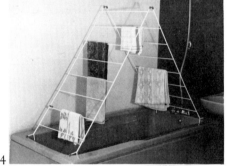

1

2

4

3

Whether your laundry is dealt with in the kitchen or the bathroom, clothes driers in a one room home must be compact.
1 The Hoover Spinarinse deluxe model D3012, which has a pump and a timer, will spin clothes iron-dry. The lid cannot be opened while the tub is spinning.
2 A tumbler drier is a boon if you have nowhere to hang wet clothes. The Eastham Burco D676 will run for up to two hours.
3 The GlenDry is a compact cabinet clothes drier with fitted rails for hanging laundry. The two-heat control gives 1·2kW for drying and 0·6kW for airing. By Glen Electric Ltd.
4 If there is no other space available, clothes can be dried on a clothes horse over

the bath. The Super Family 16 Drip Dryer by Auriol Ltd is made of plastics-covered wire and folds flat when not in use.
5 The Power-Lectric Blow Dry is an automatic wall-hung clothes drier. Laundry is hung on rails in a zip-up polythene bag and drying times can be pre-set from 15 minutes to two hours at two heats. When not in use it folds away against the wall.

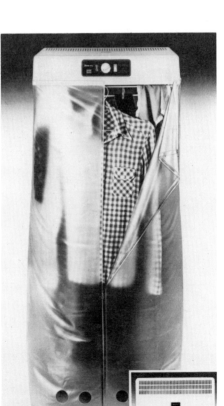

5

conditioning. In kitchens, which are frequently connected directly to dining or living areas, cooking fumes can be extracted via a cooker hood. The most efficient type is ducted to an outside wall – a fairly expensive structural job – but you can get reasonable results from the charcoal filter type that cleans the air and returns it to the room. The main drawback is that they tend to be noisy. Extractor fans come in many shapes and sizes. They need careful siting, for a fan in the wrong position can actually aggravate the problem. However, most reputable manufacturers provide clear instructions as well as an advisory service.

If you have a bathroom or lavatory without windows, building regulations not only insist on ventilation but specify the size and type of ducting to be used. Even bathrooms with windows can benefit from some additional ventilation. In some cases louvred windows will provide sufficient air circulation – but they can be draughty too. Again, extractor fans, either window-mounted or ducted into the ceiling, will help to remove steam and condensation without draughts.

Keeping the home fires burning
Being comfortably warm is rapidly becoming a luxury in itself with the rising cost of fuel, but warmth is really an essential and increased expense has only encouraged the homemaker to consider the question more carefully. What has emerged from the energy crisis is an emphasis on saving heat from going to waste and this in turn has drawn attention to the importance of good insulation. Insulation is simply the process of wrapping up and sealing our bricks and mortar shell to keep the heat in and the cold well and truly out. If you own your own house you should, if you're installing a central heating system, also invest in a sound, money-saving insulation scheme. Heat can be lost through roofs, walls, windows and doors, and each of these

needs to be insulated in some way, according to the circumstances. Roofs and lofts can be made draught-free with polythene sheeting and then insulated with glass fibre quilt or mineral granules. Windows can have heat losses through them reduced by double glazing – either by installing new, hermetically sealed window units or by adding a second glass layer. Walls, it appears, account for most heat loss and recently a lot of attention has been given to this area. Cavity walls can be given an insulation filling, inner walls can be faced with insulating boards and so on. For major improvements like these it's best to get advice from the specialists in the field – some jobs you can do yourself, others are more complex.

People living in a single, rented room will usually be unable to make major changes, but they can still seal off draughts and cut out the cold by smaller measures. Ill-fitting doors can create horrendous draughts which can be reduced by fixing draught excluders to their bases as well as a plastics foam strip around the frame. Windows can also have the draught strip treatment, keeping out dust and dirt at the same time. I have seen polythene double glazing fitted over a complete window as a cheap, temporary measure. Good heavy curtains will help to keep the cold out and the heat in – one over the door keeps draughts out as well. The traditional 'sausage dog' draught stopper is still a useful weapon in the fight for warmth and can look quite attractive into the bargain. Walls and ceilings can be insulated to some extent quite inexpensively with polystyrene sheet or tiles, but do remember to use the proper adhesive and don't cover them with gloss paint or they will be a fire hazard. Floors are also responsible for losing heat. Fitted carpets and thick underlay will obviously help, but if a bare painted or sanded floor is your lot, draughts can be cut by filling in the gaps with wood fillets or wood filler.

Heating

The ideal heating for an open-plan space is a central heating system that can be controlled within specific areas, as with a conventionally divided house. This controllability is needed simply because you will want more or less heat in different areas depending on what you use them for. Kitchens, for instance, need a low level of background heat, whereas you will need to have a higher temperature to feel comfortable when just sitting around and relaxing, and sleeping needs something between the two. The choice of heating system will depend very much on the type of fuel you have on tap or can make room for – for instance, you need a good deal of storage space for both solid fuel and oil, whereas gas and electric systems can be contained quite simply. The choice of system also depends on the house concerned – its size, shape and style – as well as the occupants' lifestyle. In fact, heating specialists claim that each case has to be treated individually. It's advisable to get information and details from every possible source before making a decision – appliance manufacturers and fuel suppliers as well as establishments like the Building Centres and The Design Centre.

For many one room dwellers the heating appliances will have to be portable, or at least movable, since any permanent fixture will have to be left for the landlord when they leave. Gas fires and wall-mounted electric heaters are fixtures in this sense, but they can be taken away with you if they're replaced by the original fitting. Modern gas fires, in particular, are so efficient and cheerful that such a performance may be worthwhile – they are also neat-looking and fairly cheap to run. Wall-mounted electric fires are neat and clean, but more expensive to run at present.

For more permanent homemakers, storage heaters are a sensible idea. There is now an enormous range of smallish models that are far less conspicuous than their forerunners. Storage heaters are

1

2   3

A selection of neat fires, gas and electric.
1 *The Glow-Worm Sonnet gas fire has pilot ignition and produces almost 2·75kW. It can be wall mounted or fitted in a hearth.*
2 *The Valor Unigas radiant convector fire*

has a 3kW output. It needs no chimney, just a flue, so must be fixed to an outside wall.
3 *The Belling Bantam 502 free-standing electric convector heater will work off a 13 or 15 amp power point.*

popular because they provide a constant source of heat on the cheapest, off-peak electricity. One recent model has a useful innovation in the form of a control that gives more or less heat as it's required, saving fuel on milder days. Other models have built-in fans that distribute warm air quickly around the room when required, in addition to background heat – a boon for people who are out all day.

There's a lot to be said for the pleasant heat and cheerful atmosphere provided by a solid fuel fire. In the long term it is worth investigating the possibility of heating your water and maybe running a radiator or two from a single fire by means of a back boiler. Coal fires have come a long way since the 'tiled surround' variety and you can now combine good looks and efficiency with that inimitable visual warmth. The main drawback with solid fuel is where you keep the stuff – particularly in a small space – and of course they do need cleaning out periodically. If you live in the country, wood may be an alternative.

Oil heaters have been flat-dwellers' favourites for some time, mainly because – despite all the increases in oil prices – they're still relatively cheap and efficient. The points against them are that paraffin has to be bought and carried, it does smell a little, and the business of filling and lighting is a bit of a bore. Today's models are a vast improvement on original designs and conform to very strict safety regulations. They look attractive and one manufacturer has added an automatic ignition device. One thing must be stressed for safety reasons, however, which is that any fire of this sort must be kept well cleaned and maintained and never moved when alight.

Most bed-sit dwellers will only want to buy small, portable heaters that they can plug in and then take away when they move on. There are vast numbers of portable heaters on the market that come in no end of shapes, colours and sizes as well as power ratings. Fan heaters are

probably the most popular now – they blow the hot air into the room and consequently warm it up faster than an ordinary 'bar' radiant fire. Both, unfortunately, are quite expensive to run. For constant background heat, plug-in convector heaters are slim enough to fit neatly and inconspicuously into any room and plug-in oil-filled electric radiators have thermostats and are useful for just taking the chill off a room.

Heating and heaters for bathrooms and kitchens need to be carefully considered from the safety point of view. They must be sited well out of reach and one useful type is the long, slim infra-red heater that can be fixed to a wall and has an angled reflector to direct the heat downwards. One neat device combines a fan heater with a light – an ideal choice for a small bathroom.

Lighting

Skilful lighting can completely transform your room. Unlike natural light, artificial illumination can be adjusted and moved around to create just the right mood and light for work, viewing, relaxing or just doing nothing at all. Work areas, quite obviously, need good, clear, overall light with some kind of directional light source: concealed strip lights for the kitchen area, maybe, or a spotlight that can be adjusted to aim the light in the right direction without causing dazzle. Living-room lighting is a little more complex, for the numerous activities that take place within this single space demand a much more adaptable system. Lighting in the dining area, where the focus is on eating, can come from a centralised pendant with a rise and fall fitment to give concentrated light over the table when you need it. The living area, however, will require a greater variety of fitments to allow for the extraordinary selection of pastimes we manage to squash into these general-purpose rooms. Ideally, you need a good, concentrated light for reading by, plus general, softer lights for

relaxing and entertaining. If you start off with a central light fitment, as most of us do, you could loop a long flex across the ceiling and suspend the fitting low over a coffee table or beside a seating unit. Clear reading lights, situated just where you need them, could be in the form of movable standards supporting spotlights, whilst a general aura of soft light comes from a sporadic arrangement of well shaded table lamps. You may not want so many different light fittings or possibly you haven't enough sockets to cater for them and are happy with the existing arrangement. It's a very personal decision and your specific requirements, even the experts claim, can only be worked out by experimentation until you arrive at the ideal.

If you live in one room, lighting can also do a lot for the decoration, for with a skilful system you can change mood and space emphasis at the flick of a switch. In open-plan areas, especially, the lighting of various 'stages' creates the visual separations that make for a greater variety and interest. One lighting specialist has drawn an analogy between the home and the stage, claiming that each function and feature demands its own individual lighting as in the theatre. A newly built or converted open-plan area will probably have been wired up to cater for this type of lighting, but most of us have to put up with using the existing fitments and sockets and improvise within these basics. In these circumstances, a dimmer switch is invaluable. Even if you're lumbered with a central light, you can then reduce its power to a hazier glow.

All the basics talked about in this chapter are more or less essential for comfortable living. You may elect to go for a major investment, or you may simply want to make small additions to an existing set-up. Whatever your commitment it's always worth consulting a specialist and shopping around until you find the right vital ingredients that will make a happy and comfortable home.

Splitting the difference

It may seem ludicrous to want to divide up a one room living area when all the advantages of open-plan – the light, airy spaciousness – could suffer as a result. It seems to be human nature, though, to want cosy intimate spaces and special slots for one's different daily activities. An even more important factor is the need for privacy if you are sharing your single space. The idea behind open-plan, after all, is not really to have everything in full view, but to gain more space either physically or psychologically by disposing of walls, corridors and doors. It's interesting to note that in open-plan offices designers actually provide divisions in some form or other – screens or walls of plants. Within these artificially created cells the occupant often attempts to personalise his or her allotted space.

The pressures, of course, aren't quite the same in your own home. You probably don't need to box yourself in to be able to concentrate, but you may need a little more privacy or cosiness than the living space provides. Dividers, apart from isolating different functions, can also give a flat, featureless room extra shape and some interesting visual stimulation. They can also add the surprise of stumbling across some different view in a hidden corner. According to their function, divisions can be as flimsy, temporary, decorative or as structurally permanent as one wishes. Quite obviously the kind of structure or arrangement will depend on the length of your stay and on what you're actually allowed to do by law or by mutual agreement with the landlord/lady. If your stay is short-term you won't want to get too heavily involved in great expense or physical effort, whereas if the room will be yours for some time it could be worth considering some kind of permanent improvement.

Dividing lines

Dividers of any sort – walls, split-level floors or simple, visual barriers – work especially well where they have the space to show off. The ideal areas are the sort you find in old Victorian houses or in converted churches or warehouses – generally not in the run of the mill bed-sitter. Dividers can, however, do their job well in any space provided that the overall desired effect is considered properly at the outset.

If you really think about all the activities involved in one room living you can't help but recognise the number of unsightly, irrelevant but nevertheless functional spots that are better hidden from view. If you cook in the same room that you eat, sleep and entertain in, it's reasonable to want some sort of split between these assorted activities. Otherwise you may find yourself sleeping and eating amidst the sight and smell of the stacks of dirty pans and dishes that can so easily pile up while preparing any meal. Eating and relaxing can often go happily together whilst sleep, although involving about eight hours unconsciousness, can often require a psychological change of mood or even scenery – it depends again on your priorities. For some open-plan dwellers it's cooking that should do the disappearing act, and if washing and bathing are part of the one room set-up, it will certainly need a comprehensive camouflage trick.

Quick splits for bed-sits

Bed-sits are usually a temporary go-between and I use the term here to differentiate between the traditional one-room temporary home and the larger single spaces that have been designed specifically for open-plan living. But temporary dwellers need their home comforts as much as, if not more than, anyone else, though any improvement or addition should either be easily taken with you or cheap enough to leave behind. Bed-sits, as the abbreviation suggests, are often small spaces where you sleep and sit, often in and on the same piece of furniture! As long as neither function is decoratively intrusive, like the introduction of a frilly bed cover, they get on well together. But if you also have to work in the same small space, you may decide that the additional clutter this introduces is too distracting and unattractive and must be screened off from the rest of the room. If you refer to your lifestyle list you should be able to see at a glance just the way you live and consequently the way you should organise your home.

Furniture arrangements

Visual dividers – and that really means things that trick the eye into accepting a symbolic partition – are the easiest and cheapest method of creating separate areas. One simple and obvious way of splitting up space is to use existing furniture in cunning arrangements. If you arrange your seating in a good conversational 'U' shape, for example, the seat backs will form a barrier between one activity and the next. It works in a similar way to turning your back on a crowd of people – you're still there but not totally involved. Other items of freestanding furniture can be used in similar ways as dividers. A bank of drawer units or a sideboard placed across an open space will provide useful storage and divide the space without actually reducing the feeling of spaciousness. Larger, taller pieces of furniture arranged in the same way can make a more positive partition. This use of large items of furniture is extremely helpful for partially or totally obliterating equally big and shapeless pieces like the bed. Even if you just put one wardrobe at the foot of the bed, you'll have created enough of a diversion for the sleeping area to be regarded as very separate.

If you're working with several multipurpose storage units, you may have to plan your 'wall' more carefully in order to get the storage in the right place to service different areas. If your partition is to run between kitchen and eating area – or dining and living spaces – you'll need to design the arrangement with one

LA MAISON DE MARIE-CLAIRE/PEROUSE

Shelving trimming a sofa is not only practical, but it is also an extremely good way of psychologically separating one activity from another. Here this sturdy,

freestanding shelving barrier creates just the right frontier between eating and relaxing without actually losing the feeling of light and space.

unit facing in one direction, the next in the other. Of course, if you have a number of units to play with, you could put them back to back and form a very thick and capacious storage wall.

If your room is devoted to work more than to play – whether study, cooking or sewing – the indispensable table could become the divider. Round, square or oblong, if it's placed centrally or running across between different areas, it will form a kind of psychological barrier. This ordinary, functional item of furniture is often the central focus for many an activity, and becomes an area that family and friends will gravitate towards. In many bed-sits the limited space forces the bed to take over the sit, and beds are such boring looking lumps. A reshuffle of existing furniture can often result in a rather stylish compromise, splitting the sleeping area off from the rest of the room. For instance, if you put the bed centrally in the room and surround it on three sides with drawer units and the odd free-standing unit, you will focus attention on a glamorous sleeping/sitting well, leaving the surrounding walls free to give a feeling of air and space. Another neat answer is to butt the bed sideways on into a corner and along the adjacent wall, and then put a wardrobe at the foot of the bed to form an alcove. To complete this arbour idea, you can make a 'ceiling' of muslin or calico stretched from wardrobe top to opposite wall. Basically, it's the height of the bed rather than its length or width that often makes it an eyesore, especially in isolation. Surround it with objects of similar or varying heights and it may well blend in to an attractive scheme. One splendid way to define the sleeping area, if it's possible, is to sink the bed into a false floor so that it blends un-obtrusively while making a neat, pleasing and functional feature. Almost any piece of furniture is versatile enough to turn its back on an area, and if you find the backs ugly then camouflage them with pinned-on fabric, wallpaper, posters and pictures.

Flexible frontiers

Not everyone, especially short-term stayers, wants or is able to reorganise a room with a furniture reshuffle. An easier solution is to have something that can go up quickly, look good while there, and be as easily rolled up to take away. Even more settled inhabitants might prefer the looks and lighter qualities of flimsy see-through partitions. A tried and tested divider designed for privacy is the good old screen. Its opened concertina shape can add a new dimension to a room that seems flat and dull, and it will cut down on draughts at the same time. Some of the nicest screens are to be found in junk shops and jumble sales. These are very often Victorian left-overs, their panels covered with embroidery, fabrics or paper scraps that depict the fashion, style and news of that period. New ones are also pretty, especially the openwork cane type that have a tantalising 'now you see it, now you don't' quality. Plain felt or hardboard panelled screens are good for anyone who wants to personalise a space – you can sew or glue on your own personal favourites and memory joggers. If you want a screen to be part of the total room decoration rather than a temporary gap-filler, you could have it covered in a fabric or wallpaper to match your overall scheme.

Not a very original divider, but still an effective one, is curtaining. As a room divider a curtain hung from the ceiling is best made up in a sheer type of fabric that lets the light through. It can be made of ordinary cheap muslin or the more expensive furnishing net – the kind of continental 'sheers' that look laddered. A more solid material is better for curtains designed to conceal storage or small working areas, and if these are hung on chunky curtain poles they can make a good-looking feature. Alternatively, an amazingly easy and colourful curtain can be made from felt. You simply cut equally spaced holes across the width, the same diameter as the curtain pole, and

A sturdy screen can provide just the right device to separate essentially private areas. This conventional screen has been fitted with triangular shelving for practical storage as well as providing a prettier viewpoint.

ANN WINTERBOTHAM

30

then slide the curtain on – felt doesn't fray so it needs no finishing. Bead curtains, for all their romantic connotations, are still a very functional way of concealing an unattractive view. Quite recently the bead curtain has made a comeback and consequently there is a good range to choose from – some of the prettiest are made of brightly coloured glass-like strings and can be bought in varying widths to fill your gaps.

Finally, a mass of house plant greenery can do a lot to divide up spaces visually. Just think of the effect spring greenery has on a dull winter garden and what a brightener potted plants are in a small backyard. To create an effective barrier indoors, you need to group together all shapes and sizes of plant – large bushy types to establish the line, smaller ones at floor level to add softness and maybe a few hanging from the ceiling in pots or baskets to complete and fill in the gaps. Try to mass them together, as one or two plants dotted here and there often look weak and ineffectual. Plants are covered in more detail on pages 57–59.

Visual tricks
Trickery in room decoration is often not used to its full extent. Basically it's the art of deception and applied to the bed-sit or single room it's often based on that well-worn saying 'what the eye don't see, the heart don't grieve over'. One good way to provide camouflage is to invent a focal point so that all eyes are directed towards it alone and skip over the immediate and distant views. Tricks like this are much used in restaurants where you obviously want your attention kept to your own table and its immediate surroundings. If you've listed your priorities and worked out your daily life pattern, it should be easy to assess which area you should highlight.

Creating a focal point isn't as difficult as it sounds. It's simply a matter of choosing your best features and then ex-ploiting them to the best advantage. If you love giving dinners to friends, for instance, but are slightly ashamed of the cooking facilities, your focal point should be the table laid to look stunning and lit with candles – no one will look any further. If the presence of a bed in the living room makes you uncomfortable, draw attention to something more glamourous – an enormous oversized display of dried grasses maybe, or shelves of interesting objects. Contrasting colour and pattern in the room decoration can also be used to highlight specific areas. If you create an arch of pattern in the centre of a plain coloured room, your eye will automatically fly to this area. Likewise with colour: an aggressive colour can't help but be the scene stealer. These are simple and cheap tricks and you can find more examples of the effects of colour and pattern on pages 60–77.

Another cunning method is to split the room up by clever lighting. Ideally you need flexible light fitments like spotlights, table lamps and rise and fall fittings with lots of switches, dimmers and light sockets for truly versatile results. One ingenious idea is to have a curtain track fixed to the ceiling that's used to carry a light fitment to wherever it's needed at the time. The flex is threaded at intervals through the track hooks and secured firmly to the end hook. You then merely draw the light across the room as you would your curtains! If you look at your one room home as you would a stage, and recall how every person or movement is accentuated by being spotlit, you should be able to work out your own lighting plan. Obviously the area you want to focus on will be spotlit or well illuminated while the places to be overlooked should be in shadow. Good and effective lighting can be difficult to achieve, though, and often the best results come from trial and error, with quite a lot of trial before you find the best result. See page 27 for more ideas and for a complete guide to this complex subject read Derek Phillips' book *Planning your lighting* in this series.

Folding doors make excellent flexible dividers and today's designs are comparatively easy to fit into any space. Here they illustrate (above) how to shut off the sleep spot from the living/dining area and (right) how to hide away neatly the distractions of kitchen clutter and debris.

Permanent measures

If you enjoy living in your one room and intend to continue life this way, you may want to install permanent dividers. Doing everything in the same space tends to overwork the furnishing decorations, so if you're planning any permanent divisions it would be prudent to tackle it all properly at the start – it's likely to look better and last longer. The kind of structural dividers favoured by open-plan advocates will usually be the ones that shut off the working and private areas like kitchens, bathrooms and maybe bedrooms. Often a wall of good-looking doors is preferable to a vista of pots and pans.

Louvred and panelled bi-fold doors that concertina as they open can be hung from the ceiling joists and fitted with a guiding floor track. These make handsome dividers that open easily, and being ceiling hung means that any minor variation in floor level can be easily overcome. They can also be hung where you please, at any distance from the storage or working recess that you're trying to conceal. A system of sliding doors works in a similar way, the difference being that the tracks allow overlapping. The advantage of the sliding door system is the wider doors and the smooth surface they provide on which you can apply your own personal decoration – paint, paper or fabric. Used over a complete wall this sliding door arrangement can look neat and be easily manoeuvred.

Alternatively, you could use the same type of track to hang a central screen dividing the room – if you fill the centre of the frame with net or muslin it could look rather Japanese in style. A sturdier but still see-through panel could be made of decoratively cut-out hardboard panels – this way you get the best of both worlds, the pleasant light plus a definite partition. See-through partitions like this made in interesting materials can easily become an attractive feature of the room. Set in a frame and fixed firmly to the ceiling, wall and floor, they also make a fairly sturdy separator. Common or garden trellis, for instance, looks lovely spanning a large, light room and can't help but introduce the pleasantly calming atmosphere of a conservatory. Rows of angled, overlapping wooden slats fixed in the same way make an intriguing divider, for although you can't actually see through them you still get shafts of light breaking through.

Roller blinds and fold-up Roman blinds are also becoming a popular answer to every problem – concealing or dividing. Hung from the ceiling, they make very flexible room dividers; used to conceal a work area or some storage, they provide a very adequate veneer of respectability. Roller blind designs are now so varied that there is something on the market to suit most tastes and styles. There are, however, do-it-yourself kits so you can make your own to match or blend with your overall decoration scheme if you can't find an off-the-peg one that's suitable. Roman blinds are slightly more tricky to make, but are worth the trouble, for when they're fixed their pleated concertina appearance looks very smart.

Clever and calculated planning of furniture and spaces allows this bedsitter to take all the day's activities in its stride. The sitting and relaxing area is designed to turn its back on the dining/work spot, while the sleeping space slips neatly behind sliding doors during the day; the result – an appearance of both neatness and spaciousness.

33

Split levels

Varying the levels of floors and ceilings is a dramatic and unusual way of creating a more interesting view within an open space. And if you have to take a step up, or the ceiling is visibly lower, you will psychologically accept this change as denoting a change in function and mood too. A simple way to raise the floor level is to build a wooden dais over the existing floor, using the existing joists to support the new structure. This can be simply a platform made from planks rested on and fixed to timber cross members – it's definitely a construction job for someone with a little carpentry experience and a lot of common sense. On the other hand, if you want your raised floor level to incorporate an undulating seating arrangement, you can build a similar structure using foam slabs and squares as the base. These will provide a flexible seating system that can be altered to suit occasion or mood. Raising the level of a floor obviously needs a room with a fairly high ceiling, partially to comply with building regulations and also to maintain the visual balance of the room.

A sensational group of plants and foliage, a perfectly and beautifully set table, plus a small but nevertheless emphatic barrier between cooking and eating, turn this very busy room into a delightfully relaxed space.

LA MAISON DE MARIE-CLAIRE/DIRAUD

If you want to lower ceiling levels you will again need a room that is higher than average. The advantages of dropping the ceiling are not only decorative ones. It can provide some valuable storage space and room to house the ugly electrical attachments of downlighter fitments. Ceilings can be lowered quite simply by fixing a wide shelf from one wall to another, supported on battens underneath and fixed at intervals to the ceiling above. You can get an interesting look by using wooden slats to straddle the span underneath, or a simpler and certainly cheaper method is to stretch fabric across the width.

There are innumerable ways of introducing different heights and depths to an open space – the choice will be based on cost, your own preferences and the room itself. Anyone lucky enough to find a room with a lofty ceiling could well afford the space to build a high sleeping/ relaxing platform, or, at a grander level, a mezzanine floor or gallery for eating, working or whatever. Obviously a permanent structure like the last two examples requires the necessary planning permission and usually professional building techniques (look at the previous chapter for specific advice on just what you're legally allowed to do). A high platform is a little simpler and can be built by a competent do-it-yourselfer with a good DIY manual. It's basically a wide shelf structure amply supported by sturdy uprights, usually at the four corners. Scaffolding – industrial or display types – makes a good, versatile support for this type of structure.

Sleeping aloft converts this very narrow room into a cosy, workable bed-sit home. The platform and the decoration designed to incorporate it add character and distinctive shape to the tight space.

JERRY TUBBY/ELIZABETH WHITING

Spacemakers

However efficiently you divide up your room, it's inevitable that doing everything in the same area is going to demand a measure of discipline and a number of compromises to make it work effectively as a 'home'. Ideally, if you were starting from scratch, you would design the complete area to be dual-purpose, instantly adaptable at the flick of a switch. But I'm sure if you had the space, time and money to follow a futuristic idea like this through, you would end up with an amazingly efficient, but fairly boring, room. Small multi-purpose homes do, however, benefit from the odd bit of flexible furniture that is able to do a neat disappearing act when required. Sensible fold-ups, flap-downs and roll-aways, if correctly situated, really do help to save space and make room for other equally important activities. It's not difficult, though, to get so carried away with the ingenuity of these innovations that you find daily life becomes a round of pulling and pushing, lifting and dropping, which makes every task impossible and living rather tedious. An overworked area like this will probably either drive you mad or straight back to your old single-purpose furniture.

Sensible planning is really the only answer. You need to work out carefully what space you need for what activity, decide which multi-purpose items would be of the greatest use to you, and finally map out the actual space they may take up in the room itself.

Another consideration, and one that's too often overlooked, is your daily routine and the routes you take to get from A to B within your restricted space. Economising on space in one direction is absolutely pointless if it causes inconvenience in another area. Space saving, however, is big business and manufacturers are quick to jump on the currently fashionable bandwagon. Many firms and individuals are producing sound and interesting ideas that are worth buying or copying more cheaply for yourself.

Cooking area

The kitchen area is probably the most difficult to arrange in a one-room home and I have to admit that planning kitchen space with a place for everything, positioned in just the right spot, is a challenging venture for anyone. However, the constant desire for ease and time-saving has resulted in many extraordinarily imaginative kitchen innovations. Kitchen planning is dealt with on pages 14 to 20; for the moment space-making refinements are the focus. In most cases, manufacturers' refinements really do save space and are sufficiently simple to operate to justify their existence, but as an aside, I must again stress the importance of convenient positioning.

In some of the 'fitted' kitchen ranges the extras offered really are a boon – a pull-out or flap-down ironing board, for example, can make you face a boring job much more willingly, especially if the board is as easily folded away and the iron is kept close at hand too. If you're lucky enough to own a food mixer you may also long for one of those special contraptions for it inside a kitchen cupboard. I personally think they are a waste of space, and really don't regret the few extra seconds it takes to take out the appliance, assemble it and plug in. What I definitely do approve of are those hideaway garbage bins – the ones that miraculously lift their lids as you open the door, or even the ones that consist of disposable bags topped with a flip-up lid. If you can afford a waste disposal unit you will find this an even more valuable labour and time-saving device.

Whether you're buying gadgets or essential cooking utensils, always select ones that stack, pack flat or make use of spare wall space. Kitchen scales, for instance, can be wall-fixed and fold up flat when not in use. You can wall-mount can openers, too, and bottle-top openers can be screwed to the underside of shelves. Another good investment is a towel rail – either the three-pronged, wall-fixed variety or the pull-out type you get as a kitchen fitment. Finally, one new idea is a lidded electric cooking hob where the lid flaps down to serve as an extra work surface and give a neat appearance in a compact kitchen. Apart from its looks, the hob is safe too – there's no chance of putting the lid down on a working ring, for a mechanism connected to the lid automatically cuts off the electricity supply. A few more simple space-saving solutions like this and our homes would work like well oiled machines instead of the cranky nightmares that we've too often come to tolerate.

A neat cooking unit for small kitchens is the Belling Formula, a retractable hob with four radiant rings. When not in use the lid folds down to provide an extra worktop, and cuts out the electricity supply for safety.

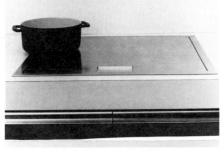

Dining area
In single rooms the dining space is often the area dominated by a table and chairs and used for work, sewing and cooking preparation as well as eating. If this is the case, you'll have to decide whether a permanent table and chair arrangement is essential or whether their daily disappearance could make the room space more convenient and pleasant. Getting rid of chairs is really quite easy these days as so many are designed to fold or stack. Whatever your price range, you should be able to find really good-looking dining chairs that are simple to fold, and likewise you can find attractive stacking versions – a far cry from those canvas community hall classics. Canvas garden chairs and campaign chairs are also good buys, for they are comfortable and yet sufficiently upright to give your back the support it needs for both dining and relaxing. What you must always remember is that even though your chairs are stackable or foldable, they still need to be stored somewhere. A design that folds flat can be hung quite easily on the wall when not in use – in fact, if they're thoughtfully placed they can look rather attractive. Even straightforward, rigid dining chairs can release floor space if hung on the wall from strong, chunky hooks, and these too can look quite good. Many of today's stacking chairs look so handsome one on top of the other that it's quite possible to leave them on view. If, however, you really can't bear the sight of your empty chairs, don't make the mistake of hiding them inconveniently far away.

Tables really are wasteful of space. They take a great chunk out of the room leaving the floor space underneath empty, and you can't really fill this space in if you want to dine or work in any comfort. Folding tables are, of course, the simple answer so long as the folding procedure really is simple and trouble free. In one of my back-to-basics homes I introduced a no-nonsense folding decorator's trestle – this, I decided, was going to be the answer to everything. It was a good, sturdy, hard-wearing table – and it needed to be for it was never folded or put away after the finger-pinching struggle of the first and last performance. A trestle table is still a good investment, but in retrospect I would have doctored mine, cutting off one end and hingeing it on a batten fixed on the wall. It could then have flapped up out of the way and, clipped securely to the wall, it would have been a very neat space saver. A similar solution for the solitary mealtime or study area is a lift-up flap screwed to a wall and supported with a hinged prop fixed underneath the work surface, and yet another idea is the table top that either slides out or pulls down from a storage unit. The surrounding space caters adequately for the nearby storage of china, glass and cutlery, and some designs offer wider shelf space that acts as a serving area. Slotted into a bank of matching units, a flap-down table top like this blends any individual activity neatly into the whole scheme of things.

Gate-leg tables – the free-standing sort that flap up into service and collapse when the supporting legs are slid away – are a good way of reducing a fairly wide diameter down to a mere few inches. If you're on your own, it's probably best to keep a gate-leg butted up against a wall and only extend one flap when you need it, as they can be quite heavy to move out to the centre of the room. Slightly more manoeuvrable are the kind of temporary folding tables that are meant for an evening's card playing, or garden tables that are specifically designed to fold quickly and easily – to cater, no doubt, for our unpredictable weather.

A piece of furniture with endless possibilities is the trolley-table. These are like the traditional wheeled trolley but are fitted with flaps or pull-out sections that provide a table top. Some are even more sophisticated and independent with their own pull-out seating. A less complicated version is a trolley that splits into two separate occasional tables – ideal for snack meals at floor level. For tele-maniacs it's a respectable improvement on TV trays; for people living in one room it's an ideal way of making flexible use of limited living space – with your meals on board you can choose where you want to eat without the inconvenience of stumbling to and from the kitchen. The original trolley itself is still a useful item, especially for less formal arrangements, and there is a design that has removable trays that are always useful for handing food round. If you entertain friends to meals often, you could find an electrically heated trolley a boon. These have heated tops and compartments that are designed to keep food warm rather than cook it, and they work fairly efficiently, certainly cutting down on the legging to and from the stove. The good thing about any 'dinner wagon' is its versatility – in fact, anything on wheels is invaluable when space is short. A redundant trolley, for instance, could easily be painted and go into service as a mobile TV stand, work surface or plant holder.

Eating in bed-sits tends to mean lap dinners. For anyone happy to sit on the floor, a multi-purpose low-level table will make a very adequate eating surface. A stunningly designed table and seating arrangement that I've seen worked so well and added such glamour and style to the simple room it was in that it is well worth including here. Basically it was a 1·2m square table that slid under a seating/sleeping dais at the end of the day. As the illustration shows, it was made from two squares of plywood with a cruciform support separating them into four storage segments. The lower sheet was fitted with castors to make the table easily movable when not in use.

Left: A trolley is a useful piece of furniture in a bedsitting room as it will double as a table or storage unit. The T trolley by John Alan Designs has a solid wood frame with white plastics laminate shelves.

Living area

Relaxing and entertaining are the main pursuits that are supposedly for the 'living-room' section, but as I've said before, one-room homes have to cater for every activity. Apart from storage, which is discussed in its own chapter later on, the major item of furniture for this area is seating. Quite honestly, in the normal single-space home a conventional sofa and side-table arrangement just doesn't work for it looks disjointed in an already divided scheme. Modular seating units are really the answer at the moment, for they give you the freedom to alter the shape and mood and can look either relaxed or formal. I think the most versatile seating units are the ones that you can buy or make yourself from size-related oblongs and cubes of fabric-covered foam. With these you can build up shapes like building bricks. You can, for instance, cover the complete area and add backrests and hollows where you need to sit – one place for television viewing, another for listening, and yet another for conversations. The permutations are endless. Even a sleeping area could easily be provided by a spread of these seating blocks forming a nestlike well free from draughts and disturbances.

You can of course opt for the more conventional type of units that actually look like seats rather than loose foam slabs. They're obviously not quite as flexible but they still provide the basis for individual planning ideas. Quite a number of these units unfold to become beds, which is a definite plus in bed-sits or small homes. Convertibles – which is what these sofa/beds are called – can nowadays be found in any style, price or size. Most are good looking and convert quickly and easily but check before you buy that the process really is simple. Some stay ready made-up which makes going to bed and getting up much more simple. If you are to sit and sleep in and on the same piece of furniture for any length of time it's really worth spending

Above: The Sleeper Sofa by Martin Sylvester is a casual strapped sofa which opens up to provide a spare bed for emergencies.

Below: The versatility of modular seating makes it ideal for bedsitters. These smart units are from Martin Sylvester's Sofa System.

quite a lot on the best-made item. When buying an easy chair or sofa you should certainly sit on it in the shop and check the following points: is the seat the right width so that your back is supported and legs hang comfortably over the edge? (This is one of the major problems with a convertible since a bed is ideally wider than this comfortable seat width.) Does the angle of the back feel right and does it give enough support to your neck? Is it covered in a durable fabric that will withstand spilt coffee or the occasional dropped cigarette?

In most seating spots you'll need an 'occasional' table – a surface of some kind on which to put books and coffee and all those other things that accumulate during a relaxing evening. Try and find one that doubles up to provide extra storage space. For instance, there are some really colourful kids' toy drums that I think would make very sturdy table tops – lift off the lid and there's plenty of space to be filled and some seldom-used heavy items will increase the drum's stability at the same time. Some tables are designed specifically to do a double job, and tables fitted and kitted out with sections for sewing equipment and so on are perfect if you need that sort of divided-up space. Tables with a storage shelf or cupboard below are also a good space-saving idea, but the glass-topped kind can look a hopelessly untidy jumble. Nests of tables, too – those stack-into-one designs – solve the need for an occasional extra table top without taking up too much space in the normal daily use of the room. In a similar vein are the new, square, lightweight plastics tables that build up into a column. These obviously save space, but if the tables are in constant use they can be more trouble than they're worth. If you own about four of these you could use them in different combinations to make up any shape of table at a moment's notice. Another good idea of this kind is a table that makes a quick change from dining height to coffee table level, simply by rearranging its supporting structure.

When you're buying or making any sort of unit furniture – tables, shelving, drinks cupboard etc – always see if it would make life a little more convenient if it is designed to pack up neatly against a wall when not in use. Movable units are particularly valuable in a small space. Space savers for storage are those low cabinets that can be used individually or banked together. These can house records, store drinks, correspondence or books, and grouped together they can perform the double duty of extra seating and a display surface for treasures. A cheaper and just as useful version of this basic idea is to use those cheerful, coloured plastics wheeled trucks for toy storage. These are large enough to hold bottles and glasses, records or needle-work, and they can be pulled around the room to wherever they're needed. Lined up they look neat and attractive too.

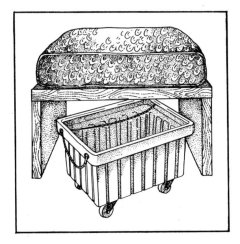

These types of two-faced furniture are a boon in cramped spaces, but only if they change function easily and quickly. When you're contemplating buying, don't get carried away by sheer ingenuity – test it and if it's a cumbersome business to convert it, think again.

Bathing and washing area

One of the newest ideas in bathroom fittings are neat modular units and there's no reason why you shouldn't top your existing lavatory, bidet or linen basket with some neat squarish lids – it could well give you space to sit and dry feet or make up your face, manicure or whatever. Showers, because you bathe standing up rather than lying down, obviously save space and could be the answer to a bath-roomless flat. One manufacturer produces a shower designed to go into bedrooms and bedsits that expands to full shower cabinet dimensions but retracts into a neat cupboard only 240mm deep. I think vanitory units fit into the space-saving category too, even though they often take up more room that a standard hand basin. Fitted basins – for this is what vanitory units really are – provide tuck-away space beneath for all those messy toiletries and cleaning materials and also

provide a counter-top where any prettier boxes and bottles can be displayed.

For quite some time bathrooms have done duty as part-time laundries and for many bed-sit owners who do not have the use of a garden, the only way to get clothes dried and aired is to hang them over the bath. Efficient launderettes have relieved the constantly dripping load to some extent, but there's always the odd hand wash that can't be done by machine.

Left: In a tiny bathroom, or a bedsitting room with no proper bathroom, a shower saves not only space but also water. The Conseal Mark 3 Foldaway Shower opens up to a full-size shower cabinet, but when not in use folds neatly away to look like a 240mm deep cupboard.
Above: A vanitory unit can hide unsightly appliances and turn a dressing table into a laundry area. Here a washing machine and tumbler drier are concealed by brightly painted doors.

This chapter is deliberately packed with ideas to help you liberate and use your given space to the full. You couldn't and shouldn't try and fit all of them into your home. Choose the ideas that relate to your lifestyle, or use these suggestions as inspiration for original space-saving ideas of your own.

Sleeping area

Ingenious dual-purpose ideas in furnishing obviously aren't limited to bed-sits and open-plan rooms. For some years, designers have been spurred on by the nagging threat of smaller homes and budgets forcing householders to spend less on their furniture. Economical, space-saving ideas were demanded and one of the first areas to get the treatment was the bedroom because this space really was ill used. The first and most useful move was the introduction of fitted furniture that provided the storage space not only to house the usual clothes and make-up, but also to accommodate a sewing area or washing and ironing cupboard.

One of the best systems is a self-assembly one that has doors, ends and sectional pieces with optional storage extras like pull-out wire or plastics baskets, shelves and hanging rails. If you could do with this kind of flexible storage within a unit you've inherited, the drawer and shelving fitments can be bought on their own and quickly installed. These really do relieve innumerable storage problems. Rented accommodation quite often doesn't provide these up-to-date units but something a little more 'characterful'. There is nothing worse than poor clothes storage space – it can't help but encourage untidiness. If you don't have enough hanging space, you could fit a very neat arrangement that accommodates about seventeen coat hangers but miraculously folds away to a depth of about 24mm and is an ideal filler for a spare alcove. Alternatively, if your alcove already serves as a wardrobe, you could use an easy pull-out hanger – quite a number of coat hangers will slide neatly away with this system. Blanket boxes and old trunks may not sound like space-savers but they provide an enormous amount of storage and can quite easily do double duty as bedside or occasional tables and seats. Tatty old trunks can be painted or covered with wallpaper to look respectable.

The best blanket boxes, I think, are the unfinished whitewood type that you can decorate to please yourself and to blend with the rest of the room.

Bed manufacturers have now latched on to the hidden storage idea as a launching point for their new models and this works in our favour. In bedsitters a bed that will disappear or conceal bedding during the day is a good and sensible purchase. Beds can now be bought that will fold away and disappear into a louvre-doored cupboard, or fold up to form the back of a free-standing bureau unit. The new classic, immensely popular with design journalists and one-room livers, is the single bed that bends in half and turns like magic into a rather good-looking coffee table. Innovations from manufacturers who have stuck to producing beds that still look like beds include simple pull-out storage drawers in the base or the easy lift-up divans that reveal capacious spaces underneath for bulky items like suitcases and blankets – all those things that one uses occasionally but that all too often sit under the bed or on top of the wardrobe. If sleeping and seating occupy one and the same space, these accessible storage spaces make chameleon-like changes so much easier. Sensible bedding like a duvet – that

marvellous continental invention – is the best answer for a really rapid transformation. If you sleep on a sofa/bed, the duvet is easily folded and hidden in an under-bed drawer, and then just as easily retrieved at bed time.

A conventional bedroom item that many people can't live without is the bedside table. In any space, this should be one of those movables I talked about earlier. I think there's hardly any home that can afford the luxury of a piece of furniture that has the single duty of bearing the early morning cup of coffee or the odd book. A bedside table could quite easily accommodate your make-up, for instance, and if on wheels it could be moved to the best light for putting on your face.

2

A bed which folds away or provides storage space beneath it is a useful feature of any home, not just a bedsitting room.
1 The Slumberland Storage Divan has a completely hollow base which is ideal for storing clothes, blankets and bed linen.
2 The Relyon B2 Bureau Bed, a full size single bed by night, folds up into the back of a bookcase/desk unit when not in use. You simply revolve the unit on its castors according to your needs.

1

3 *The Relyon Table Bed has three uses: by day a smart coffee table or a foam-seated stool. By night, it becomes a single bed, using the foam cushions as a mattress.*

4 *A custom-made foldaway bed provides the ultimate in camouflage in this stylish one-room flat. It has been decorated on the underside with chrome strips to give the*

appearance of a wall mural when not in use. Designed by Rothermel Cooke.

Storage

With space being at such a premium for people living in one room, it's not only essential that furniture should be as multi-purpose as possible, but also that there's a place to keep everything out of the way when it's not needed. Storage space – or rather the lack of it – is one of those nagging problems that troubles everyone in our rapidly shrinking homes. As one of nature's natural hoarders, one in fact who can't resist adding more 'can't live withouts' to an already bulging space, I feel well qualified in discussing the subject.

The ideal storage system is one that tidies away everything you don't want to gaze at or be confronted by – items that are ugly but essential or that need protection from dust and damage – and yet keeps it all within easy reach. It sounds a lot to ask, in terms of both design and looks, but it is not really quite such a daunting problem if, like everything else, it's thought out and planned properly from the start. Living in one room means that the storage you install has to be versatile enough to accommodate the enormously varied shapes and sizes of every item you use and wear. Most manufacturers of storage units, though, tend to produce units that are fitted out for a particular purpose in specific rooms. Living in one room, if you want continuity of looks and dimensions, it could be a question of adapting the shell of your selected units to suit your needs, or alternatively, improvising your own system.

If you can find manufacturers' units that will house all your possessions and you are able to run them along the length of the room, using all the vacant wall space, then you should be home and dry. This is the ideal answer – to be able to use free wall space for all your storage, streamlining what would otherwise become a maze of clutter. But whether you can afford to install new units or whether you're lumbered with existing pieces, the problem of slotting things away in the appropriate and convenient space is just the same. There is nothing more likely to drive you mad than a stupidly small storage unit that's inconveniently situated. If you can grasp the simple and obvious basics of storage planning, you should find that you can reorganise your home to run more smoothly and efficiently.

Planning principles

Planning your personal storage really means harking back to the original lifestyle chart plus a complete inventory of the things you own. It is a horrifying thought but a well worthwhile project if your living space is small and overworked. Once you know what you need to house, you can then work out how and in what space. Planning perfect storage is simply a question of listing, measuring and allocating space for all the items you want to store. You should decide how frequently they will be used – annually, monthly or daily – and position them in the most convenient and ordered way. It's logical that the infrequently used items – like spare blankets and suitcases – should be placed at the extreme top or bottom of the storage area, and likewise that the well-used daily items are put at an easily accessible level, with don't knows somewhere in between. As a final caution – when planning the total volume of storage, the rule is if in doubt to allow more rather than less!

Each area of your one room will have its individual planning problems, and it should help first to run through these different requirements and then give some idea of the various types of storage available to deal with these demands.

Cooking area

Planning of any sort is partly a matter of personal preferences and in the kitchen I think this is particularly true. No two cooks work in the same way and I'm sure this is why too many are claimed to spoil the broth. I love my kitchen, and everything for me is right at hand, but whereas my hand may stretch for a liquidiser, another's may reach for a potato masher. Whatever the size and arrangement of the area, there are always some basic planning points to remember. The ideal working system is one that runs neatly between the processes of storing food, washing and preparing, cooking and serving, with as much worktop as possible between the activities. Above and below these specific work areas you obviously need to store items that relate to the particular function. It's logical, for instance, to position pots and pans close to the cooker and oven – maybe beneath a hob or to one side of a cooker. Likewise foodstuffs – tinned or dried – should be stored by the preparation spot. It is also reasonable to have your other food store – the fridge or larder – close to the preparation area. Crockery and cutlery, if kept in the kitchen, should be at the end of the line – near the serving area and dining space.

An idea that's becoming a much accepted storage formula in the kitchen is drawer storage for everything – even pots and pans. It is, in fact, a surprisingly

logical method of storage and pulling out a drawer is certainly preferable to groping into the backs of cupboards. Wire mesh and solid drawers are now designed to contain everything in the kitchen – deep ones for pots and pans, shallow ones for tins and vegetables, pull-out racks for crockery. The only consideration here is to make sure that you have enough room to pull drawers out and that the plan of the units doesn't mean you have to edge around the drawers when they are pulled out. Good storage doesn't necessarily demand expensive equipment – a very adequate and easily accessible system is a bank of vegetable rack trolleys slotted under a work surface or a row of those remarkably versatile storage boxes on wheels. If cash is even shorter, use wooden storage cartons fitted with the sort of roller-skate wheels normally used on heavy fridges and cookers to make them easier to move.

There are, of course, many individual refinements like this – how and where to store each item virtually. You can find many more examples in the *Planning your kitchen* book in this series.

The living-room
In a single-space home, the 'living-room' really means the total area. However, in this section of our survey I will deal with the sort of storage space you need as if it were a conventional living-room. This room is, in every sense, the most hard-working of all spaces for it has to present immediate good looks to outsiders as well as provide comfort and familiarity for the occupants. It is the place in which most time is spent and consequently it's the most memorable impression maker. Storage for this space is slightly different from that in other areas, in as much as it's a fifty-fifty arrangement – half hides, the other half displays. Most manufacturers of living-room storage units provide hiding places for the things you don't want to show off to the world, while giving open shelving – often with subtle,

concealed lighting – to display your favourite personal treasures. This, in one form or another, is just the right balance. Complete concealment would give a barren, non-committal appearance and most people have personal prizes they are proud to exhibit.

Units like this still allow a certain amount of freedom for individual decisions as the manufacturers often provide a range of layouts or modules that can be assembled to suit your particular needs. Again, as with kitchen and all room planning, you need to measure up everything and gauge exactly just which open and closed areas are necessary to accommodate your possessions. Also think whether you need an unusually flexible system to house items that standard fitments don't cater for, like the extraordinary bust of Beethoven that's your most treasured possession or the hi-fi system that is designed for sound and not necessarily as a compact unit. Again it all comes down to logic and painstaking planning.

Sleeping area
Bedroom storage is usually easier to plan because the processes of sleeping, waking and dressing are more simple to assess, and all that's really needed is a wardrobe and some drawer space. The fitted, built-in units that have recently become popular use all of the wall space from floor to ceiling. Top spaces should house all those things that we used to sling on the top of the wardrobe or hide under the bed – suitcases, hat boxes or seldom-used things like tennis rackets or ski boots. The lower space is still usually used for clothes, but it's generally so well planned that the space allows for short length clothes as well as medium and full length items with drawers for shirts, pullovers and socks and maybe a rack for keeping shoes neat and tidy. Whether you are buying new or converting the old, the same planning patterns still apply. You really need to get out all your clothes, sort them out into

varying lengths and then measure the longest and shortest, for this will give you an accurate gauge of the sort of inner storage you need. This may sound ludicrously simple and really it is, but it can be slightly more complex if you're having to convert an old wardrobe to suit your needs. The rule in this case is to use the hanging space for all your clothes and, where the short lengths fall, fill in with extra drawers or fit another hanging rail for a second tier of shirts and skirts. Use the inside of the door for belts and ties, and the wardrobe floor for a shoe rack.

A good space saver that I can't resist for the bedroom area is the sensible notion of sleeping on top of the storage. Basically, you build a bed base, using shelves, cupboards and drawer units to act as the perimeter support to a ventilated ply base and mattress. If you choose a versatile modular system you can devise your own arrangement – custom-built, in fact.

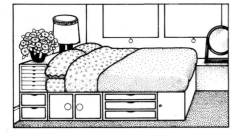

Bathing area
On the whole, bathrooms are small and compact areas, designed solely for the purpose of washing, bathing, shaving and, maybe, making up. In most cases, toiletries and medicaments will be all that need storage and a simple shelf plus a bathroom cabinet with a lock will cope satisfactorily. If you're lucky enough to have more space than most, you could fit cupboards and more shelves to hold spare towels, toilet rolls or laundry materials.

Odds and ends
Brooms, the vacuum cleaner, wellingtons and golf clubs – these are the sort of things that never really have a home. In a single room there's even less spare space to play with, unless you can lay claim to the cupboard under the stairs or you live high enough to inherit the attic. Day-to-day living is full of 'odds and ends' and it's pointless to overlook them so try to incorporate them somehow into your total storage plan. If you haven't any extra room, or you're having difficulty juggling your existing storage furniture, try and allocate a specific spot for odds and ends within the room, such as the entrance area or a curtained-off alcove. Plan this valuable area carefully, filling it with hooks and holders, shelves and baskets, racks and rails so that it doesn't just become another muddled corner.

Types of storage available
The need for tidiness and order imposed by our shrinking homes has resulted in a glut of storage notions. There are now endless types of modular units that can go into bedroom, living-room, kitchen or bathroom. Likewise, there are hundreds of fitted units – free-standing, adjustable and so on – and this large choice should provide something for everyone and every situation. To guide you through this overgrown maze, I've listed some of the best known types with their specific advantages and disadvantages.

Fitted furniture, for instance, is furniture designed to fill a given gap. At best, it is either custom-built or a selection of off-the-peg components adapted by a carpenter or yourself to fill your exact requirements. This sort of fitment allows any irregularities within the room to be disguised or shown off as you wish. On the whole, units like these are not free-standing and will become a permanent fixture. In some of the more expensive off-the-peg ranges, you get the refinements of planned storage inside and space-saving gadgets, with plinths to raise

or lower worktops and panels to fill in any small gap between unit and ceiling. These units are fine for people who, firstly, know exactly what they want and, secondly, can afford both the expense and the space that's involved in picking this type of fitted furniture. They do look neat and streamlined and, if properly selected, will provide just the right amount of storage. I feel, however, that this total look bought straight from the manufacturer can often miss out on personality and character. At the cheaper end of this market you can just buy the bare basics – the outer shell alone – and it's up to you to install more drawer or shelf space and any other fitments. On the whole this is a more flexible approach, but again you must be positive about your needs before making your selection – it's pointless to order nothing but cupboards because it seems easier if, as an afterthought, a set of drawers would be handier. Whatever the system, fitted furniture needs extremely accurate measurement. It's no good spending a fortune on some living-room wall units if the whole thing's just a few millimetres too long.

Modular furniture is an increasingly popular way of catering for multi-purpose storage. This type of system is made up from size-related multiples of a basic module – cubes and boxes, cupboards and shelves that can be built into any shape, like building bricks. There are numerous variations on this theme, ranging from the DIY cube on cube constructions to the more conventional wall of cupboards, drawers, desks and open shelves, wall-mounted or floor-standing. The great thing about this furniture is its flexibility. It allows the individual much more freedom of self expression and style. With the common module as a basis, you can mix and match any combination of open or closed units – they can climb up the wall or skirt round it – and since many are free-standing you can use a row of units as a room divider. The advantages are clear and they're ideal for

CubeKit by CubeStore is a neat storage system. Plain, white or brown chipboard cubes provide shelves, cupboards, drawers, record racks or open display units which can be built up one by one as required.

anyone who can only afford one piece of furniture at a time as they can be bought individually and added to gradually.

One of the main drawbacks with this built-up system is that it needs very careful planning. Because units are designed to grow as you wish, there is a tendency for a wall to look 'bitty' and ill balanced as you add pieces one by one. You may also find that space within the module is too tightly planned. As with fitted furniture, careful measuring and assessment of the space you really need should help you to avoid these difficulties. And a great advantage of this type of storage is that you can take it with you when you leave, so it's worth buying well made units that will last.

Shelving is my personal answer to every storage problem. Open shelving is a good-looking bonus in any room for it provides a display platform as well as easily accessible, capacious storage spots for endless books and bits. Shelves go anywhere – kitchens, bathrooms, bedrooms and living-rooms, under stairs and over doors. You can build them any width, any length and any height. Shelves, however, can be useless and dangerous if they're not fixed securely to a suitably sturdy wall or if the supports just aren't capable of bearing the load. Off-the-peg shelving systems come in several forms : you can either buy free-standing framed types that are built as a unit and make excellent room dividers, or the more common wall-mounted variety. Adjustable wall-mounted shelves are a good bet for any room where the odd bit of storage space is needed to relieve the pressure of overcrowding, but they are especially good for someone in a first home whose initial possessions are minimal but likely to expand. Shelving of this type often relies entirely on cantilevered brackets locked into a pre-slotted vertical track ; other systems use slotless uprights that allow infinite adjustment. The strength and reliability of both systems depends on the intervals of the tracks and also on the way in which they are fixed to the wall.

If you only want the odd shelf you can just buy a single length of wood – it may not fit flush if the wall's uneven but it will probably be good enough. Single shelves will usually need some sort of bracket support and the type depends on the wall behind them. Plasterboard, for instance, won't support anything and check before drilling that you're not going to cut through the electric wiring. The advantages of open shelving are clear – it's versatile and adjustable and often a simple solution to a complex storage problem. It can also be a splendid focal point in the rest of the room's decoration, filling in an awkward alcove or lining an entire wall. To my cost I know one of the major disadvantages is dust, and really there is no way round this. Another potential problem is tidiness – if the storage is to be seen by everyone, it really must be considered and arranged as such, and not allowed to become the dumping ground for unwanted debris from your handbag or pockets.

Click – one of the many bracket and upright shelving systems – is more versatile and good looking than some as it has no slots.

Storage in unlikely spaces

However cunning manufacturers have been in devising space-saving storage ideas, they're still battling with the perennial problem of the individual and his or her non-standard home. The secret of totally successful storage is ingenuity – finding new ways and spotting overlooked spaces to bear most of the load, and this is especially true if you're living in one room. Believe it or not, there are overlooked spaces that have potential as storage areas in even the smallest room.

Alcoves are one of the most useful spots for they can be fitted with open shelves or closed off with curtains, blinds or doors to provide the hidden space you need to protect clothes and to hide any ugly but essential items. If you want to make them a permanent cupboard, it is a good idea to choose the sliding or bi-fold doors that are ceiling-hung. These give you the freedom to decide on cupboard depths as they can be suspended where you like. Because doors and windows have always had their one obvious function, many people fail to realise their potential for other uses. In fact the space around and especially above them is often quite deceptively large and often big enough to fit in narrow shelving to provide extremely useful storage space. Visually this is effective, too, for the shelving acts as a frame for the door or window and adds emphasis to a flat and featureless wall.

An ordinary pole slung under a shelf and fitted with butchers' hooks can relieve a great deal of cupboard space if it carries awkwardly shaped pans, sieves, colanders and other kitchen gadgets.

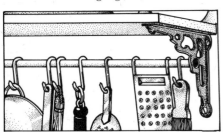

If you're looking for space to fill in, the vast area over a bath shouldn't be ignored. A stack of shelving running from top to bottom at either or both ends of the bath, at a safe and convenient height, would make ideal space for extra towels, soap and cleaning materials. A more adventurous and permanent idea is for the bath to be totally 'fitted', with cupboard space running along the length above the bath and open shelving at either end. This sort of arrangement obviously needs a largish area to prevent claustrophobia, and to allow a reasonable standing height between bath and the false ceiling created by the floor of the cupboard. Ceilings that have been lowered for visual interest as described on pages 34–35, can be thoroughly exploited for storage so long as the structure isn't too flimsy. Innumerable items can be stacked away on these lofty heights. Quite obviously if the space is open, the items will need to be reasonably neatly arranged.

Although most of us have discovered how useful walls can be for storage, few of us take advantage of the ceiling – possibly because it seems so difficult to get at. It's true that this is a problem and ceiling storage (unless you can fit it with a hoist) should only be used for little bits and pieces that need only a very occasional review. One way of making an attractive ceiling container is to create a row of fabric pockets across the ceiling, which can be simply a length of fabric supported at intervals with sturdy wooden battens.

Similarly, large draw-string sacks hoisted up by a pulley system are ideal containers for items that you're not going to need all the time. Not such a new

niche, but one that's just as valuable, is the space under the stairs. This wedge-shaped cavern, fitted out with a good light and some shelves and hooks, will house cleaning items, sports equipment or clothes, down to the smallest box of pins and sewing equipment. If you actually get around to removing the door, it could end up as an attractive extension to the living area.

DRAWINGS BY ANN WINTERBOTHAM

Ever since the storage pinch was felt, people have been pushing things into any item of furniture capable of concealing them. The classic 'under the bed' space is still a useful camouflage if the space exists, but many of today's beds are divans – sleek creatures that squat low and neatly on the floor. Fortunately, bedding manufacturers have overcome this problem by inserting drawers or deep boxes within the bed bases. Space can also often be made under or around unit seating, especially if you design and fit it yourself. Window seats, for instance, with lift-up lids, have always been invaluable storage spots. A skirting of shelving units fitted snugly around a group of seating units or a sofa is another good way of catering for odd extras.

Elevating a sleeping space, apart from looking more interesting, relieves valuable floor areas ideal for the storage of clothes, books and so on. This particular sleep spot is designed to vary in height to provide both visual irregularities as well as steps.

LA MAISON DE MARIE-CLAIRE/BESTEL

The little things that mean a lot

However 'right' you've got your basic storage, I suspect you'll find some daily essentials that have been overlooked and are constantly getting in your way. It's often the simplest idea that overcomes the problem. For instance, a simple knife rack situated at the right height near the

worktop is a well organised safety measure. Cup hooks screwed to the underside of shelves provide easily accessible storage and some pretty relief in what may otherwise be a coldly clinical kitchen area. In fact the underside of a shelf is one of the most useful and under-used storage spots. You can either fit in special slide-on wire baskets that are specifically made for this purpose, or use old jam jars, screwing the lids to the underside as the illustration shows – it makes a neat and simple storage idea that's cheap and effective.

Another thrifty but good-looking measure uses brightly painted open tins, fixing their backs to a piece of board to produce a highly individual slot-in wall storage unit – it's an idea that can be used successfully in any room with a great deal of style.

Other useful extras for the kitchen include those pretty, plastic-covered wire hanging flower baskets that make rather handsome holders for vegetables, cooking accessories or tools.

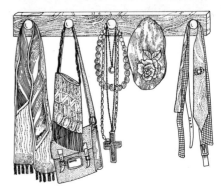

A good way to deal with other personal accessories, like scarves, beads and belts, is to hang them over painted wooden or china knobs that have been fixed to a wall batten – this way they're easy to select and become an attractive feature in themselves.

DRAWINGS BY VANA HAGGERTY

If you trim shelf edges with strong carpet binding pinned at intervals, this is another neat way of slotting oddities into place.

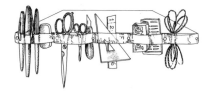

The back of a door is one of the greatest space savers for small, easily lost items, and it's generally a spot that goes unnoticed. Cupboard doors, for instance, can be fitted with racks and hooks on the inside as well as the outside, or fitted with flush panels of peg-board – thin hardboard punched with small holes for hooks or pegs – to hold tools, kitchen equipment or kids' stuff. The current fashion for wall-hung containers is another favourite way of making the most of a door. If you make your own fabric container, you can design the pockets to house just what you need to store – shoes, belts, handkerchiefs or kitchen scissors, aprons and cleaning materials. The container can be made to fit within the frame of the door and hung to suit your height.

A similar do-it-yourself idea is to sew chair panniers to hang over the arms of an armchair or sofa – these are very useful for holding papers, knitting or your current book, and save the space usually needed for a table.

The last place where space is often underused is above and around the lavatory. Narrow shelving built around the pipes and cistern makes room for extra toilet rolls, books and magazines, cleaning materials and the odd plant to make the area more alive and attractive.

Necessity must still be the mother of invention for storage ideas, for the really satisfactory living arrangement is still hard to find. It is these individual inventions that make all the difference and mean that every small home is essentially personal for its owner.

Style

Homes, of course, are much more than just boxes full of boring essentials. They reflect a personal statement of style, the indefinable ingredient that makes every room individual and can be summed up as total individual taste. For convenience, decorators put styles into the different categories of traditional, cottage, ethnic, modern and so on, but living in one room, especially if it's furnished by someone else, will be quite a challenge to anyone hoping to create a personal 'look'. Quite honestly, when one doesn't have the freedom to decorate from scratch, it's the budget brighteners discussed on pages 68–71, and things like cheap, idiosyncratic furniture, that give a room a personal stamp.

Below: Lack of clutter plus neat furniture arrangements can often create an impression of modernity, whereas a jumble of junk-shop treasures haphazardly arranged (right) will conjure up a feeling of cosiness and character.

BILL MCLAUGHLIN

Junk shop treasure

It's in the early stages of homemaking that people tend to patronise junk shops in search of cheap, essential pieces of furniture. Later, when you begin to realise that these relatively inexpensive items are often better made and more characterful than a modern purchase in the same price range, the regular visits can become a mania. If it's your first experience of furnishing with second-hand furniture, you need, firstly, to learn how to spot a bargain and, secondly, to decide what to do with it. To be honest, there aren't that many bargains around, especially in the normal run of furniture,

that will slip straight into use in the cramped spaces of our modern homes.

Items that are still worth buying, in spite of their recently inflated prices, are pieces like marble-topped wash stands. If the bottom isn't too good, you can barter for the top for use as a pastry-making surface. If, however, it turns out to be a perfect piece, then you've purchased a characterful item that will make a stylish side table in living, dining or bedroom. Heavy, over-decorated Victorian dining furniture shouldn't be overlooked, for its heaviness looks rich against the new, dark colour schemes, or it can look positively bizarre if painted in bright colours. A

popular buy at the moment is the over-mantel, that amazingly ornate concoction of mirrors and mini-shelves that used to stand proudly over the fireplace. Today, its extravagance is being used to decorate bedheads, bathrooms, hallways – in fact every room where a flat wall surface cries out for ornament. It seems that almost anything can be resurrected: redundant birdcages make comebacks as hanging plant holders; travel trunks return for duty as blanket boxes, hi-fi hideaways or as extra seating; and particularly pretty cast-iron cistern brackets return to support shelving.

Bargains these days are more likely to be found in what seems over-sized and over-decorated furniture, and they will probably only be bargains if you're prepared to use a little imagination and work on a conversion treatment. Huge Victorian wardrobes, for instance, can be taken apart to make a number of smaller, useful pieces: the base drawer section turns into a separate chest of drawers or the foundation for a seating arrangement, whilst the top can remain as a more reasonably sized wardrobe/cupboard. Or you could, of course, take off the usual mirrored door and hang it on its own as a wall mirror, using the remaining timber to make shelves and cupboard doors. Genuine, old-fashioned desks can be dismembered to form separate narrow drawer units and a solid table top, and the small, pigeon-hole sections can be used for spices and herbs in the kitchen. Not a new idea, but still a valid and attractive one, is to use the decorative metal stand of an old sewing machine as a base for a table. If the drawers themselves are still sound in a chest of drawers that's falling apart, then they can make good, wall-hung boxed shelves, and the surplus wood and spare knobs can be kept aside for use else-where. Old kitchen tables, the sort with a knife drawer section, and also table top desks that have side drawers, make magnificent coffee tables if the legs are cut down to a reasonable height. Old doors that you may be able to pick up off building sites or out of rubbish skips (a valuable source of timber and treasure) can be used to make dividing screens or cut in half for cupboard doors. Redundant flush panel doors make splendid dining tables or work surfaces, though it is a good idea to support them on wheeled drawer units or second-hand mobile filing cabinets to help in moving them around.

Second-hand office furniture shops are also a wonderful source of reliable and functional pieces, and so long as you can imaginatively repaint and decorate them, they'll never resemble the cold grey horrors of the office. Filing cabinets with their deep, capacious drawer space can be used anywhere. They're ideal for all types of clothing and, because the interiors can be wiped clean, they're just as capable of storing vegetables and food-stuffs. You can sometimes find old library trolleys, too, fitted out for storing books and files, and these make marvellous, flexible shelving systems. Stationery cup-boards, apart from their use as wardrobes, are good for storing those hopeless, home-less items like tennis rackets, brooms, laundry bags, ironing boards and so on. But the best office furniture, I think, is the solid wooden stuff, for however battered the exterior appears, it can always be sanded down or sufficiently well prepared to provide a lovely surface to seal, stain or paint. Multi-purpose rooms need versatile furniture and a standard office desk with a pull-out type-writer section could provide just this. If you fix casters, it can become an in-valuable, flexible item giving you work surface, drawer space and a work exten-sion. The nicest item I ever bought from an office supplier was a tilt and swivel chair – I can't believe anyone could make such an item redundant, for its classic looks and comfort are perfect for work.

Cane furniture also fits well into today's homes for it's light in both weight and looks, and it's also still quite cheap. Cane and bamboo was used in Victorian

times for the most extraordinary items. There were hall stands with hat and coat hooks and mirrors, chests of drawers and cupboard units, as well as the more obvious conservatory tables and chairs – a whole roomful could look quite effective.

Antiques to add the finishing touches are not especially good 'bargains' today, for as fast as good antiques leave the country, our sources of latterday junk are being upgraded to fill the voids. You can, however, still sometimes find the odd bargain in the collection of disputables and doubtful taste items that's often found hidden away in odd corners. The 20p jumble boxes in second-hand shops are precious sources of kitchen utensils and cutlery that often look better and have a longer lifetime than cheap new ones. Odd plates can be bought cheaply too – mainly just because they're odd – and if you stick to one colour theme, your odd collection could look like an original intention. Vases, ornaments and pictures, true indications of personal style, can also be found at fairly reasonable prices in so-called antique shops. Quite honestly, it's difficult to state what's a bargain, for one man's treasure is another's rubbish, and the best buys are often the ones bought simply for personal pleasure and enjoyment.

Cleaning up junk
The art of buying true bargains in second-hand furniture lies not just in finding unusual and handsome pieces, but in selecting sound and sturdily built items. Always check over the pieces you're interested in carefully, and look for damage that could be irreparable or might need costly, expert attention. It's unlikely that you'll find any handed-down furniture that hasn't incurred a small amount of damage over the years, but if it's the odd chip or wobbly leg, these can be easily remedied at home. If damage appears to be more extensive or you spot too many tell-tale holes of wood-worm, don't touch it. Some of the items

you find may still have a fairly presentable surface that could be left in its original state, possibly needing only a thorough clean and not much else. If, however, the structure is sound but the surface rather damaged, you'll have several alternatives, and these are all, unfortunately, hard work.

French polishing isn't easy and is certainly not a quick re-vamp job, as it involves laborious preparation. First you have to remove any build-up of old wax, then give it a thorough scouring with fine wire wool, and then more cleansing and so on. Makers of French polish provide clear instructions in the hope that they'll be read and followed. Stripping down to the wood involves just as much graft and mess. Proprietary strippers will take off any number of coats of paint and varnish and the process is fairly simple. Again, as always, read the manufacturer's instructions thoroughly first, and if in any doubt, consult your local DIY shop. Most suggest that you should wear rubber gloves and I endorse this, for if you consider that the solution is going to remove layers of paint, imagine what it'll do for your hands. The usual method is to paint on the stripper, leave it for about ten minutes for it to start working, and then remove it with a scraper. It's quite a long, hard job. When the surface is clean, any holes or imperfections in the surface should be filled. As with any finish, the perfection of the top coat relies entirely on the preparation of the base surface. A thorough sanding job, starting with a coarse grade paper and working up to a fine grade finish, is the only way to achieve this smooth base. It's then, at this naked stage, that the final finish has to be decided upon – stain, varnish or paint.

You may be so pleased with the surface you've uncovered that you decide to leave it 'natural', sealing or waxing it to give a protective surface. If the bare wood isn't too attractive, you could colour stain it or simply paint it. Again, the process of building up a good surface is as lengthy as the removal of the original layers. With paint, the build-up is basically primer, two undercoats, sanded between each, followed by a fine top coat. Modern polyurethane stains are ideal for they colour and seal at the same time, but sanding with fine sandpaper between coats is still necessary for a really fine finish.

Old cane furniture has built-up dirt in all the cracks and most of the crevices, and as you might imagine this is difficult to remove. Whether you simply want to restore it to its original colour or to prepare it for painting, cane must be scrupulously cleaned. It's a chore, for you have to apply a strong detergent solution with a paint brush between all those irritatingly interwoven strands, and after that it then requires a final and thorough rinse. If you intend painting your cane, it's easier, though less economical, to use spray paints as they apply coats evenly, even in the crevices.

Metal office furniture, likewise, needs some preparation for a good final coat of paint. Most office pieces are given a factory finish originally, and will smooth and clean quite well with steel wool soap pads. Follow this with a rinse and final cleansing wipe with turpentine or white spirit, and the surface should then take paint well.

Gilding the lily

Some of the second-hand furniture you find will be sufficiently decorative to keep its original looks, others may become more exciting with an up-to-date paint or stain treatment. Today's best buys are often the sound, utilitarian pieces that looked frightfully dull in their day – and they can still look equally boring if left as found. Decoration of any sort can work wonders, however, and can be tailored to suit the mood, humour and style of the owner. There are innumerable easy ways of brightening up and personalising these stalwart items apart from the straightforward coat of colourful paint. Regular

geometric designs such as stripes and squares can look strikingly effective, and require only the patience needed to mask off carefully the areas not to be painted, to paint the exposed areas, allow them to dry and then repeat the process all over again. It takes a great deal more talent to create your own design and paint scenes freehand. You may not get the same satisfying feeling, but you can get a similar result by copying designs onto graph paper and carefully transferring them onto the subject. You can also cheat with amusing, pictorial ideas by simply photographing your subject, projecting it on to the item of furniture and then painting in. The skill here is to decide on a subject of the right proportions to fill the given space. Stencil designs are comparatively easy to apply and can effectively create neat borders and panels. Get inspiration from familiar objects around you like plants, fruits or embroidery, wallpaper and fabric designs. Draw the design onto card or, even better, a vinyl tile, cut out the shape and you've a template that you can paint walls and furniture with again and again.

GEOFFREY FROSH

In your own home, however, the choice of type, the position and arrangement is all yours – and so, of course, is the challenge.

Choosing the right type of plant

Easy-care plants will generally do well anywhere and are the answer for anyone who's not tremendously interested in horticulture but loves the look of plants. Aspidistras – those large, dark green leaved plants that were Victorian favourites and are enjoying a revival of interest today – are good low-level fillers and will live almost anywhere. Most types of ivy will also survive anywhere, though they can be difficult to start and like most plants they're not too keen on gas fumes. Spider plants (chlorophytum) are the classic display plant for office, home or anywhere. Their stripey leaves and hanging young plants are good softeners for shelves and corners, likewise trailing tradescantia. Mother-in-law's tongue (sansevieria) is another good survivor and its strange, spiky growth is an attractive addition to a multi-plant arrangement. Fatsia japonicas are quick growing, bushy types of plants that look handsome and fill a large space quite inexpensively, and geraniums are also easy growers and make banks of colour from spring to autumn as well as maintaining interesting greenery throughout the winter. You could also consider rubber plants (ficus) and the very decorative swiss cheese plant (Monstera deliciosa).

Dark corner plants are invaluable for any home where areas without light need covering up. Again, ivy of all types will twine its way around decoration problems. A particularly interesting version is Fatshedera lizei, which is a cross between ivy and Fatsia japonica, resulting in a smallish but handsome plant. Kangaroo vine (Cissus antarctica) and grape ivy (Rhoicissus rhomboidia), often only distinguishable by their size of leaf and growth, are good in shady situations because they can climb up walls, over

Natural decorators

Greenery, both indoors and out, is one of today's simplest and most inexpensive decorators. Its versatility stems from the variety of shapes, sizes, colours and textures that can be found in the different types of household plant, and it's all these that enable you to alter, define, accentuate, soften or hide specific features. I suspect, though, that plants are popular not just because of their decorative value, but because of the sense of achievement and creativity that one gets from keeping the contrary creatures alive and well. To

get an idea of how to use plants skilfully you should look at magazines and interior design books to see how the experts carefully site plants to liven up their schemes – to draw attention to a particularly lovely feature, to soften hard outlines or to fill dull corners. You could also note how plants are used in public and commercial buildings, where they are designed to create a sense of calm, as well as to provide barriers between different work areas and tokens of civilisation in the often extraordinarily de-personalised buildings constructed for us to work in.

obstacles and consequently disguise any number of oddities. Ferns, such as maidenhair or asparagus ferns, are obvious plants for shady spaces, and are especially good in bathrooms that have moist, humid conditions.

Sun lovers are often colourful, flowering plants that are only too ready to fill windows to the brim, making 'conservatories' out of the dullest rooms. Fuschias and geraniums are colourful sun lovers and their varying hues will brighten and cheer up almost any viewless room – likewise busy lizzies (impatiens), which flower feverishly throughout the growing season and sporadically during the winter. Coleus, with its exciting, multi-coloured leaves, is another good and cheerful addition and as a contrast to all these brilliant colours, you could introduce the delicate, white flowers of passiflora. The classic sunshine lovers, of course, are the cacti and succulents that thrive naturally in the desert and, cleverly grouped, these can form a mini-desert within your window frame. Mini-palms like neanthe also make good, long-term window decorations.

Plant care

The secret of success with any plant is to care and learn about it. Most nurseries supply care tags with their plants and these give a very good survival guide. Rule number one is never to buy a plant just for its looks alone, and rule number two is to decide at the outset where you want it to live and then scrupulously to select the size and shape you want within the range that's suitable. The increasing popularity of house plants has resulted in flourishing garden centres and nurseries in most towns and these usually have a wider selection and better advice than the traditional flower shop. On the whole, the care needed is minimal: plants need to be watered possibly two or three times a week in summer, once or twice every fortnight during winter months – basically watering when the soil looks dry. A fine

spray is good for most plants. They also need feeding from time to time with liquid food during the growing season – spring to summer. Apart from this basic, essential treatment you'll need to clean the leaves occasionally – either with leaf-shine for glossy leaves or simply with a damp cloth. As I mentioned before, plants appreciate a constant temperature and consequently they aren't too happy when shut off from the rest of the room's warmth behind closed curtains, or positioned too close to the window glass, which can cause scorch damage to the foliage.

ROB MATHESON

Decorating with plants

If plants are to be an integral part of the design of your home, their looks, shape and size quite obviously have to be considered as carefully as the choice of a wallpaper or colour scheme. Because plants have such strong, individual characters and looks, you need to choose a variety that will blend in with your

particular style or way of furnishing. A small and cosy cottage-style room, for example, would be overpowered by a strong, large specimen like Monstera deliciosa. Smaller hanging plants like Ficus pumila, or a window arrangement would be much more at home. Stark modern interiors, though, cry out for large, dramatic plants with extravagant looks that add to the impact of the interior. The art of designing with plants, as I've said before, is to know how they'll grow and what they'll do. Tall, tree-like plants can be either used on their own as a feature or as a centre for a large, multi-plant group. Small, neat pot plants are good ornaments for shelves, window-sills, or as soft edgings around a large formal arrangement. Climbers and trailing varieties, as you may imagine, are invaluable for flowing over hard edges, creating a climbing cover for blank walls, filling viewless windows or for simply twining around pipes or over ugly pieces of furniture. Hanging baskets, too, are a useful and attractive way of adding interest to eye-level space. Flowering house plants are often used to add colour to an all-green arrangement or can be used in groups or singly to heighten and accentuate a colour theme in the rest of the room's decoration.

On the whole, a collection of plants grouped together has greater impact than individual blooms sited at random around the room. Grouping plants successfully is a skilled business. Visually, they need to be an interesting blend of textures, tones and sizes, and you need a strong, characterful plant to give the height, with bushier types to fill out the arrangement and small plants to shade in the edges. The skill, of course, isn't just restricted to the choice of foliage, for you also have to select plants that can all live under the same conditions. For inspiration, look at some of the professionally styled groups found in many reception areas in public buildings; for advice, turn to reliable reference books. In single rooms, plants are often the easiest items that you're either allowed or can afford to introduce, and they can really alter and improve matters drastically. For example, they have always worked wonders as camouflage: intrusive pipes, as long as they're not hot, can look positively enchanting with plants rambling over their stark frame. Even those gaping holes of redundant fireplaces become quite fresh and inspired when filled with greenery. Climbers can be trained to grow round doors and windows to create the effect of an arbour, while hanging plants can be positioned to trail off shelves, over viewless windows or down stair treads to cheer up the dreary haul home. Bleak, non-committal areas like hallways appear a great deal more welcoming with a softening of foliage and blank corners become quite important if filled with a substantial specimen. Plants, in fact, are remarkably flexible, and used confidently and considerately, they will add interest and warmth to any dreary spot.

Miniature gardens within the living area are fascinating both to look at and to create, and they could well turn into an absorbing hobby providing the gardener with endless hours of interest. Some mini-gardens are true miniatures, designed specifically to imitate the larger, outdoor variety. These are often made in troughs or bowls, planted with miniature trees and small growing plants interspersed with rocks and pebbles to form land shapes and paths. As with any plant group, a good foundation is essential: you need a sound layer of pebbles or stone to provide drainage, topped with good soil. For the arrangement you'll need small trees to add height and structure, plus low-growing alpines and rock plants to form the covering, selecting each plant for their balance of colour, texture and shape. These little patches really are fun to plan and grow, and they make an impressive and attractive household decoration. Mini-gardens can also be rustled up by grouping together a number of common or garden species that might look

GEOFFREY FROSH

insignificant on their own, to make a splendid bank of greenery. If you own a collection that will live happily together, they can be planted out in the same container. Otherwise they will need to be separately potted and then assembled in a trough or plant box. Good and attractive containers for these 'gardens' are Victorian wash bowls, earthenware crocks or large, enamelled laundry basins, or today's neat, fibreglass or plastics containers designed specifically for the job.

Bottle gardens have a particular fascination for many people who are charmed and intrigued by the puzzle of how the plants ever started growing in this enclosed space. The best and most popular container is the carboy and consequently these are becoming increasingly difficult to find. There are, however, some other good-looking bottles that are just as suitable: large flagons of cider and double litre bottles of wine, for instance, or you could try shop-sized sweet jars, fish tanks or bowls. Creating a bottle garden is basically the same as constructing any mini-garden – soil is introduced through a paper funnel, plants are bedded using long-handled tools worked carefully through the bottle neck (ordinary domestic spoons and forks lashed to a garden cane will do extremely well).

Because the plants are enclosed, the atmosphere within the container tends to be humid, so that water is needed less frequently than with normal house plants. Use small growing plants that like humidity and need the minimum of watering, like bromeliads. Window boxes, both indoors and out, help to create a view and provide a soft frame to a bleak outlook. In a good sized box, about 20mm to 30mm deep, you can grow herbs, little bushes, salad or just beautiful blooms to climb around and fill your window. Outdoor boxes obviously need to be firmly secured to the sill to prevent a disastrous and dangerous fall, and this is also a reasonable precaution for indoor versions. It takes only a small amount of thought and planning to keep your home green, tranquil and flourishing all year round.

Decoration

Decoration, contrary to the common opinion, is not just the icing on the cake. Ideally, any home improvement should be planned thoroughly through all its stages from the outset, with the colour scheme, patterns and textures carefully chosen to blend with or accentuate particular features that already exist in the room, or that are to be constructed in the new scheme. This may sound simple and desirable, but for many of you reading this book, your one room bed-sit is probably already decorated by the landlady or else your budget won't allow many costly improvements and brightening ideas. In this event, quick camouflage tricks should not be over-looked. This chapter is for people allowed to personalise their room with their own choice of colour and pattern, for those of you establishing an open-plan space, and for all those others who can only afford to make some small, but crucial improvement to their lot.

Choosing the right colour scheme

The decoration of one of my many bed-sitters should go down as a classic. The landlady, whose pride and joy was the cleanliness of her rooms, was also either fanatical about fire-engine red or mean enough to suffer us poor tenants to a cheap job lot. In my very small, very bed-sit room, this blast of red was admittedly cosy, but the solid colour proved visually exhausting. The shattering colour scheme just didn't give in, for as one fell into the haven of bed and sleep, you lay back to focus on more of the rosy hue defining the ceiling rose. Obviously outsiders who don't have to live in the space can be insensitive to the impact of their cheap job lots. Fortunately, if you're working out your own colour scheme, you can easily remedy any odd over-enthusiastic statement of personality if it turns out to be incompatible with day-to-day living.

The art of decoration is to choose a scheme to create the right shape, size and mood for your space. What you have to decide first is when you use your room most – day, night or both – and whether you want it to appear cool and neat or warm and welcoming. What you use the room for is also important. It's clear that a vibrant, wrestling decoration idea just wouldn't be suitable if you need a clear head for studying. On the other hand, a very cool colour scheme could encourage lethargy. If your home fits into the larger open-plan category, with many different functions, you can use colour and pattern to outline the boundaries and accentuate focal points, although it's important to treat the area as one space in an overall scheme. Though they may seem confusing, these points really do matter, for the effect of colour in our lives is an emotional and powerful one. The wrong colour, however striking it might appear on first viewing, could turn out quite impossible to live with.

Qualities of colour

Colours fall into two categories: warm and cool. It really is true that what is known as a cold colour can give a cool, if not chilly, feel to a room. The colours on the cold side are white, blues, greens and some tones of purple and lilac. Red and its close associates like oranges and yellows all throw out heat. There are, of course, degrees of temperature intensity within this framework. Each colour, depending on its mixture, can go hotter or cooler – look at any paint colour chart and you'll get the idea. See how the appearance varies within different shades of the same colour. Light is also crucial to colour theory and rooms themselves can appear hot or cold depending on the direction of the light source. As a rule, a northerly facing room will get cold blue-grey light whereas a room facing south has the advantage of noonday sun. Although full sunshine is never guaranteed in this country, it is still sensible to balance room temperatures by warming up a coldly-lit room with a warm colour, and tempering sunny rooms with cool, tranquil hues.

Colour really is a marvellous free ingredient that can add an enormous amount to a room if used with care and skill. As well as varying in temperature, it varies from light to dark, and this also influences its uses. Light shades are arrived at by adding white, and since they tend to reflect light, these shades will make a room seem brighter. Conversely, darker shades are produced by adding black or grey and, as you can imagine, these shades have the opposite effect.

When black has been added, just as at night, the colour doesn't reflect light but absorbs it. In furnishing and decorating these points are important. Light colours will open out spaces and visually expand a room whilst the darker shades will draw in the space, creating an all-enveloping atmosphere.

An all-white scheme with a small dash of colour can create all the variations of shape and colour so vital for one-space living without losing the desirable quality of light and spaciousness.

How to use colour

One of the most common tricks is to use dark colours on very high ceilings to lower them visually and, maybe in the same scheme, to use a lighter shade for walls to make the room seem larger. Likewise, if you reverse the experiment, you would make the space appear narrower and loftier. Dark colours, because they absorb light, are often useful in rooms where you need to create unity by diminishing irregularities – alcoves, doors, windows or anything that too often interrupts a clear run of wall space. A light colour used in the same situation will emphasise these features, but if the surfaces are badly pitted and the already muddled walls have odd screws or gas pipes, then this brightener could well highlight all these things that you'd really rather overlook. These are only the basic rules and like most rules they can be successfully bent and broken. But if you understand these principles of colour you should be able to appreciate and achieve the powerful results of successful colour application.

Light and dark colours, for instance, if used as partners, can create a variety of shapes and areas within the same space. If, in your one room, you want to draw attention to a specific activity, you can use colour to pinpoint it. A dining space, for example, decorated in a dark shade would appear more enclosed and intimate, while a working spot, because it demands concentration and good light, would be best decorated in white or a cool colour to emphasise its practical nature. For more examples look around at your immediate surroundings. The offices of doctors and dentists, you will notice, always look light and tranquil, so that you feel they're clean and confident. Restaurants, on the other hand, are often painted in dark, absorbent colours to give a relaxed, enclosing feeling. In a quick snack bar you may well find brighter, more lively surroundings. Every colour is emotional and evokes different thoughts and memories for everyone. There are, though, some recognised colour reactions that you can use to manipulate your own surroundings. Reds, for example, are claimed to be the most stimulating colours, while blue is restrained, cool and aloof. Greens are tranquil, restful shades. Purples are bold, fairly aggressive colours, for some people they are still suggestive of mourning – you either like them or loathe them. Yellow and orange are jolly, sunny shades, on the red side more lively, on the yellow side more calm and peaceful. Neutral shades are generally used to temper and control; on their own they're non-committal and this is why they make excellent backgrounds for living-rooms where people and objects provide the colour.

Colour in one room

In a normal, divided-up house, different colours can be used for different effects within the confines of single spaces, but clearly a little more care is needed in open-plan areas. Quite honestly, I think single rooms and the larger open-plan spaces are best kept to one overall colour with small areas or features picked out in another tone of the same colour or in a sharper contrasting shade. Although you may long to fill the room with all your favourite colours, you should really try to confine it to one, or at the most, two accents if you want to preserve your original space-saving objective.

In a small bed-sit particularly, it's reasonable to assume that there's enough going on already without creating more distractions. Here it's certainly best to decorate in just one colour using its light and dark shades for any focal point or detail you want to accentuate or disguise. This of course, doesn't restrict your initial choice of colour – you can be as adventurous or as safe as you wish. But as a rule, a light shade will make the small room seem larger, while a roomful of heavy, dark colour could look and feel oppressive.

Larger rooms can get away with a lot more, for already you enjoy some space and your movements are not so tightly confined. Again it's simple, effective and uncluttered if you use tones and shades of the same colour. This needn't in any way look boring, for you can still regulate the shape and purpose of specific areas by using lighter and darker contrasts to create impact. Mono-chromatic schemes – for this is what single colour schemes are called – work even more successfully and subtly when you take textures and surfaces into account, for this is an ingredient that's generally taken for granted and over-looked. The most varied and pleasant monochromatic schemes take into account the textural appearance of the flooring, wall surfaces, furniture finishes and so on, and use them to create interest within the single colour. To do this successfully you need to blend the rough with the smooth, the chunky with the fine, the shiny with the matt – it's the play of light on these separate surfaces that creates the depths and variations that prevent a room scheme from looking flat and dull. You can get the idea if you consider how well two opposing materials can blend. Think of chrome and leather, cork and plastics, wool and glass – each surface acts as a foil for the other and consequently each appears more interesting than it might on its own.

If you want a more daring room scheme, you could liven it up by adding an accent colour. Accents, as the term implies, accentuate – so take care how and where you use them. Accent colours are designed to catch the eye and give a plain room a startling jolt. The general rule for two-colour schemes is to use one overall colour with the chosen partner for smaller areas and details. You should choose either a related colour scheme or a contrasting one. Related schemes are ones where you use colours close to each other in the

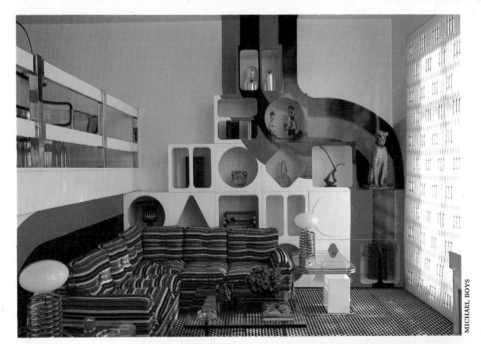

Right: Brilliant colours can be used keenly and daringly to give shape and accent to a flat featureless room, or alternatively they can be used to create a warm and inviting atmosphere in an otherwise potentially characterless space.

63

spectrum – colours, in fact, that contain the same ingredients as each other, like blues and greens, reds and oranges and so on. Contrasting schemes rely on the use of opposing colours and these combinations are often more potentially aggressive and need fairly careful handling. Contrasting colours, for example, are blues and yellows, or oranges and purples. Used in full strength they're powerful and sometimes disturbing; in degrees of shade and tone, they can be very enjoyable.

Larger, open-plan spaces need especially careful colour application. This space still has the same see-it-all quality as does the small bed-sit even though it's probably skilfully divided to cater for family life. The colour scheme here should be the same as the correct and ideal colour scheme for a conventional, segmented house. This is to use one prevailing colour and then create the various moods for different rooms and pursuits around this foundation. This overall single colour is possibly the only way to preserve the feeling of opened-up space that was the initial objective. Again this sounds like a recipe for an instantly dull and boring environment, but in fact it's a sound and space-making basis on which to build up your own personal shape and style. Within your living area, which may include kitchen, dining and relaxing areas, you could use the same accent colours in different tones to hint at borderlines, shape out different areas and create moods within each section, and yet still retain the look of space. Say the overall colour was beige, for example, and the accent green. In the calm, relaxing area, the neutral beige could be dominant with touches of green adding the flair. The working, active area could go one hundred per cent startling green while the in-between dining space could be a blend of both – dark green walls, pine furniture, green tableware and so on.

BERGER PAINTS

Above: The neutral colour scheme in this one-room space looks interesting simply because of its carefully balanced blend of textures and tones.
Similarly, the cleverly balanced, pattern-on-pattern room opposite uses all the intricacies of the many design forms to create an equally successful space, but totally original in mood and style. Living-room in designer Susan Collier's house.

TREVOR SUTTON

How to use pattern

Patterns on walls, floors and furnishings are another key variation in a disciplined colour scheme. Using pattern well adds a new dimension to flat planes of colour and will stress the mood of the room and personality of its owner.

The safe and successful way to work with pattern is to select one that either blends in with the main colour or provides the accent. The same pattern used for blinds, curtains, cushions or whatever, can't help but give an orderly and well thought out appearance. If you enjoy mixing patterns and want to use them to develop a room's style, you'll need to play carefully, for the right pattern blend can look stunning but can also be a chaotic disaster if clumsily used. Playing with patterns and getting just the right blend and effect is a skill that comes with practice. The basic rule to get the correct balance is to use disciplined designs with rambling ones, small scale patterns with large ones, and always mix patterns with one and the same pre-dominating colour. These rules can, of course, be broken, and some of our best interior decorators have done so in an extremely successful and dramatic way. For the beginner, though, it's much more satisfying to start simply and successfully and then work up to a complicated scheme with the confidence of former knowledge.

Choosing the right materials for the right spot

A major consideration in decorating, especially if it's a long-term project, is the choice of the right materials for the right application. It may seem an obvious point, but conditions in different areas really need differing qualities from their decoration materials. The areas within the home fall simply into three categories: the wet, messy ones like kitchens and bathrooms; the hard workers in terms of looks and wear like dining-rooms, hall-ways and living-rooms; and the lightly-used sections like bedrooms and, to a lesser extent, the dual purpose work/bedroom.

Bathrooms and kitchens obviously require water-resistant, wipeable finishes. At one time this used to limit us to a paint treatment for the walls, but they can now be brightly patterned since the introduction of vinyl papers, and this is a welcome step towards making these often all too clinical areas a little more cheerful. Ceramic and plastics tiles are the other, more expensive, answer if you need a steam and water-resistant surface. These can be found in numerous colours and designs but a whole tiled wall costs a lot and must be considered as a true long-term invest-ment. Flooring in these areas also needs to be easily mopped, and again today's imaginative designs and materials have made it easy to find something that's right for your particular decoration scheme whether it's vinyl, rubber, cork or even ceramic floor types. On the whole, I think the vinyls, in either sheet or tile form, are the best bet in terms of both cost and durability. It's an uncomplicated material to buy, too, for laying is fairly straight-forward and the more you pay the better the quality in terms of warmth and comfort. With rubber flooring it can be difficult to maintain its good looks, whereas cork is easy on the eye as well as on the feet, but is really quite costly. Ceramic tiles are even more expensive, and also cold on the feet unless you have adequate heating. They make a careless drop an automatic breakage in the kitchen, and you may also find that the design wears thin with regular footing to and fro.

Living and dining areas need to have sturdy finishes, too, but they should have a veneer of softness and warmth, so you need materials that are capable of bearing the strain of communal living and also of comfortable respectability. For the walls, there are simulated textures and finishes that make the look of luxury quite practicable – wall-coverings like hessian, silks and grasscloths. For many people, of course, there's nothing to touch 'good old paint', especially as the new formulas have made it so easy to clean and apply, and there are now some really smart colours and fine finishes available. Wallpaper, too, should never be overlooked. There are a number of manufacturers who are producing attractive, good quality papers that are designed for short-term use – a question of two or three years' wear maybe. This makes it so much easier to keep up with the current fashions in home decoration.

Flooring, of course, depends on the use of the rooms and, quite honestly, on the occupants. Some people may find a washable floor the quick and easy solution, while others enjoy sinking into the deep pile of a carpet – in one room you may well find it doubles as seating too. Carpet tiles are a good compromise for they come in a number of qualities, from man-made fibres through the coarse hog's hair versions and on to the more luxurious wool. The advantages are clear and persuasive: they can be loose-laid and then lifted up and replaced if one gets damaged; they can be fitted individually so you're free to create your own design; and they're available in different qualities so you can decide what level of luxury you can afford. Fitted carpets are always popular for they instantly replace floorboards with a plane of colour or pattern and the up-keep is a simple round with a vacuum cleaner. In open-plan spaces this isn't so easy, for where does one stop the 'fit'? A break can, of course, become a visual dividing line but this will only work well if the different functions really can be confined within their allotted section. The ideal, I think, is to buy a carpet square to cover an area of an all-over workable floor surface.

Furnishing fabrics also have to be hardwearing – not only to cater for lively kids but for careless adults too. Man-made fibres, at their best, can produce good-looking, easy-care fabrics that make life much simpler. The ones to look for are the stain-resistant types that can be found in ranges of tweeds, velvets and a number of patterned fabrics. Zipped and pull-off covers are extremely useful in family households as they can be stripped off, washed and replaced in next to no time. If you already own furniture with the traditional covers and wish they were more practical, you could always apply a dust, dirt and stain-resistant finish. The do-it-yourself types are applied with an aerosol spray and as they are only a veneer they will last for a limited time.

Conventional bedrooms, on the whole, get little wear and consequently can be furnished with pale shades and delicate materials. If you're lusting after a hand-printed wallpaper, for instance, this is the place to put it. Carpets, too, can be long and shaggily luxurious, in light colours, without the expense of having to pay for the 'strength' you need in hardwearing areas. But if you're living and sleeping in one room, all functions are probably closely amal-gamated, and it's more sensible to choose more practical, tough materials in a single decoration scheme for both living and sleeping areas.

Paints provide much greater freedom for total individuality. The two daring schemes illustrated here show clearly how this medium turns a normal flat wall into a true fantasy feature. Painted by Martin Sharp.

DAVID CRIPPS

The individual touch

Regardless of how individual you'd like to think your decoration is, it's usually a skilful composite of manufactured goods. Original ideas are hard to find and most of us borrow ideas, pick brains and amalgamate the information into our own individual style. One of the newer trends in decoration that works towards individualism and is virtually fool-proof, are ranges of co-ordinated wallpapers and fabrics. Co-ordinated ranges offer a number of fabrics and wallpapers that, because of their colour link and their discipline of size, style and scale, work well together. The freedom for individual choice comes from the fact that you can pick whatever combination you want, within the controlled confines of the design. The possible permutations are endless and the results can be exotic and stylish. In the same room you could paper a ceiling in one design and the walls in another, or you could accentuate one feature wall and reflect it in the curtains and soft furnishings. In true American style you could put pattern everywhere – on walls, ceilings, windows, sofas and table, and the likelihood of a major disaster is considerably lessened. Too much pattern can be claustrophobic in one small room, but a careful, well co-ordinated selection could add interest to the landlady's left-overs: a tailored bedcover, for instance, planned to match wallpapered panels that freshen up the old wardrobe, or a tablecloth to match the roller blinds covering a storage space. An exotic, and quite expensive, idea would be to drape fabric into a tented ceiling over a seating well with a co-ordinated covering. The application is truly up to you.

Ideas using paint allow for individual style too, and some manufacturers produce patterned murals to encourage householders to use their talents to cover plain walls with their own works of art. These ideas include borders of flowers, neat geometric designs and summer scenes, and you simply scale the design up from a graph to fit your wall space and then paint it in as if by numbers. Murals are not easy to conceive for yourself, nor easy to apply, so if you'd like a scenic view in your living-room, bathroom or kitchen, this method is attractively simple. Striking effects can also be achieved with stripes of colour. Lines of colour can lead your eye to wherever you want it to focus: they can define a border, emphasise a level and therefore widen or heighten the room's proportions. Stripes are not easy to apply, and you need to mask off the areas very carefully with tape, allow the paint to dry between coats and before removing the tape, and even then you may find a little retouching with a straight edge may be necessary. The results can be stunning though and definitely worth the effort. So are the many other decorative effects that can be achieved with paint like two-tone panelled doors, chequered ceilings, friezes and so on. One of the effects that's most difficult to do but immensely successful in a limited room space is *trompe-l'oeil*. This is a surface painted to deceive the eye into believing the view is really part of the room. For instance, you could paint a door to represent the view of the hallway beyond, or window shutters with a copy of the normal daily view outside. If you like the idea, you can always cheat by photographing the subject, projecting it onto the surface and filling in – again as if by numbers.

Friezes have become a current favourite for outlining and defining different areas or as decorative skirting at ceiling or floor level, designed to emphasise width and space. The wall-paper friezes now available are so exciting that they can and should be used to give prominence and style to neglected odd spots such as the side panel of the bath, around the work surface in the kitchen, or as a decorative footnote for the base of a bed.

Fabrics always add a personal touch, too, and anyone able to sew on a button can run up a cushion cover. Even the dreariest of furnished rooms can come alive with a cleverly collected cluster of cushions. In many one room set-ups, cushions feature high on the list of extra comforts, both on the floor and to disguise a bed. If they're designed imaginatively with carefully chosen fabrics, they could become a central feature of the room, giving it a lot of personal character and style. A miniscule bed-sit,where the bed is hopelessly obvious, looks much more like a living-room if the bed gets a fitted cover, and if the curtains are made to match it can look positively smart. It's the softness and variety of textures in fabrics, plus the fact that things can be made at home to fit, that makes them such a universal homemaker.

Personal touches in the flooring field are generally restricted to tiles – carpet, vinyl or lino – since they can be manoeuvred and manipulated to form patterns and paths. An edge border, for instance, looks smart as well as helping the room appear wider, or a central design creates a focal point conversational arrangement where no other exists. Hopscotch and chequerboard designs turn sensible flooring into a fun feature. Like stripes of colour on the walls, stripes of carpet can visually lead you from one area to another, useful in open-plan living.

Using mirrors is another successful decorative way to create more space: their reflective power – both of image and of light – visually enlarges a space in a way that has to be seen to be believed. This makes them an obvious boon for an open-plan area or small bed-sit, but mirrors must be sited very carefully. You should first decide what spaces you want to extend and then work out how to place the mirrors effectively but unobtrusively. This positioning is important, for if reflections become too obvious they can cause visitors some embarrassment, resulting in hurried and early departures. A dining-room I know that was treated in this way had mirrors positioned so badly that half a meal-time was spent examining personal eating habits and the other half considering one's appearance. The rule is to place your mirrors where people can't be distracted by a view of themselves. If you can't solve it on paper, walk around with a piece of mirror glass noting where the most light and the best view is reflected and also where the mirror itself is virtually unnoticed. Mirror glass is expensive and a whole wall would cost you a small fortune. Even mirrored plastics sheet is costly and it has the disadvantage of being stretchable and liable to mark easily. Small areas of glass can be applied in mirror tile form or in sheets of small mirror squares, but if applied to an uneven wall surface both of these will distort the image. A good-looking answer is to buy several old framed mirrors and arrange them as you would pictures over a complete wall span – this produces interesting reflections and also makes an attractive and unusual feature of the wall itself.

Budget brighteners

There's nothing more frustrating and depressing than living in one room, hating the sight of it and thinking that you haven't enough money to do anything about it. In fact, it doesn't take a lot of expenditure to improve your lot, and some of the nicest ideas that I've seen have come from free or fairly free hand-outs. Patchworks of any sort are classic, thrifty labours of love and patchwork today is treated as a serious craft. However, if it's a quick, face-lifting necessity that you need, you can run up a machine-worked cover quite easily. Apart from the traditional bedcover, patchwork makes characterful curtaining too, and beautiful panels for screens. Collect scraps from dressmaking friends, or from rag trade throw-out bags or by asking for out-dated sample

This smart sitting area gets most of its good looks from throw-aways. The walls are covered in redundant wrapping paper trimmed into respectability with carpet webbing, and the shiny supports for the coffee table are four nicely shaped tin cans.

GEOFFREY FROSH

Oddments of wool skilfully knitted into plain and patterned squares make a handsome bedcover and a colourful focal point for the room.

swatches in fabric shops. Patchwork carpets can be made in a similar way from shop sample swatches that can often be bought at sale time and glued onto a strong hessian backing. A much more complicated but quite stunning patchwork uses wallpaper. Pieces of wallpaper are cut out in traditional patchwork shapes and then conscientiously applied. To get the right look you must work out the design on paper first. If you have the patience, it looks unbelievable, and you could use it in a small alcove if an entire wall defeats you. If you don't have that much patience, you could collect several redundant sample books and simply stick up the pattern pieces in their original squares.

An easier move than scrounging is saving. There are many items bought daily and thrown away daily, that could well be used as free decoration. Newspapers, for instance, make a really very good-looking and quite fascinating wall surface. For a quick cover up you can stick up a week's news and be done with it; if you're more selective, you could make a wall scrapbook by building up a historical collage of a particular person or interest. Magazine scraps of favoured stars, fashions or views, cut out and carefully built up into a diary of decorative information, would make a colourful focus for any wall. Both newspapers and magazines are flimsy and will need a strengthening coat of clear gloss varnish to give them any sort of lifetime. Brown paper parcel wrapping, if well pressed and flattened, makes an extremely handsome wall finish especially if the seams are bordered with a carpet binding. Corrugated paper – the sort that's used for packaging – also gives an interesting regimented striped effect over a whole wall. This material can also make good roll-up blinds. Admittedly you have to roll them up manually and secure them with tape, but when extended they have a neat and sculptural effect. You can often buy discontinued paint

colours in sales when the paint is perfectly good but the colour, for a number of reasons, has been removed from the shade card. Odd tins of paint like this can convert a monstrosity into a masterpiece overnight, but I feel I should stress the need to choose a colour you like rather than just a bargain, and preferably a colour that works in your room. Picture frames, chairs, wardrobes and drawers painted in the same colour tend to take on the same personality and if you choose an aggressive shade – probably because you hate the furniture in the first place – you may find when painted that it's even worse. Choose a colour you like and you may learn to love the furniture too. A little paint will go a long way in one room. One small pot of paint, for instance, can produce a frieze of stencil designs around the walls or track a pattern over an ugly bit of furniture. An even better idea if you have the patience and a near perfect floor surface, is to cover it with super, large stencil designs – maybe ones that reflect the wall frieze. Painted floors are comparatively cheap brighteners. They don't keep the draughts out but they do improve the looks of the room. Floorboards can be painted individually in a spectrum of colours or in specific designs such as borders, Greek key, colour graded steps or chevrons – whatever design will live happily with you and your furnishings.

Fabrics can be gleaned from jumble sales, charity shops or friends and can be used not only for patchwork but as throwover disguises for a monster sofa, or as bedcovers. A frilly bedcover is the biggest bed-sit giveaway and should quickly be replaced by a crocheted throwover or tailored cover. Jumble sales often produce stunning dress and furnishing fabrics, and some full-skirted dresses have enough fabric for a pretty tablecloth and some matching napkins from the left-overs. Other material can be used for cushions, screen covers or cut into strips for rag rugs. Straightforward drapery stores still have bargains in hard working fabrics like calico, muslin, hessian and bed ticking – all good looking and sturdy. I've used muslin, as I explained before, to create a false ceiling. It's delicate and see-through enough to prevent claustrophobia but still create a sort of wonderland world. Hessian makes a smashing wall covering, curtains, and unfitted soft seat covers. Ticking is a less flexible material and consequently makes good 'tight' seat coverings as well as stunningly simple blinds and curtains. Calico is a delightful off-white, washable material that is cheap enough to make enormous canopies, curtains, cushions and just about everything. If its plainness worries you, it's easily brightened up with ribbons and bindings or by dyeing.

Silly and simple individual notions are often the ones most remembered and enjoyed. One very basic and barren home I visited was made instantly radiant and attractive with festoons of fabric pennants like bunting latticed across the ceiling, corner to corner. Another idea for decorating rooms where not too many improvisations are allowed, are rows of large felt and fabric banners hung from the picture rail to skirting board. Or you can make an enormous blank wall hanging of felt on which to pin your favourite scraps and personal mementoes, which would be a lovely memory jogger to take with you when you leave. A soft, enveloping effect can be achieved with shawls, especially the beautiful, heavily embroidered ones, draped over walls and ceiling to create a cavern of softness and warmth. The overall appearance and mood is like an exotic Oriental tent. Similarly, a ceiling made from lengths of fabric, looped and secured to the ceiling at intervals, makes a dull, old room a much more interesting space. Quite honestly, it only needs a little time, energy and an enthusiastic imagination to establish an individual and pleasant home.